MW00389489

One Hundred Leaves

A new annotated translation
of the *Hyakunin Isshu*

by Frank Watson

ISBN-13: 978-1939832009
ISBN-10: 1939832004
LCCN: 2012904229
BISAC: Poetry / Asian / Japanese

For information about reprints, email:
followingtheblueflute@gmail.com

Cover art for the front cover is derived from a Hiroshige III (1842/43 - 1894) print, "Murasaki Shikibu at Ishiyama Temple," printed around 1880.

Cover art for the back cover is derived from a print by an unknown Japanese artist, printed sometime from 1750-1900.

All interior artwork is derived from public domain work by Hiroshige (1797-1858), Kuniyoshi (1797-1862), and Kunisada (1786-1865).

Published in the United States of America

For a broad selection of poems and translations, please visit:

www.followtheblueflute.com

Contact Information:

Email: **followingtheblueflute@gmail.com**

Twitter: **@FollowBlueFlute**

Table of Contents

A Brief Guide to Appreciating Japanese Poetry

Around 1237, Fujiwara no Teika (1162-1241), author of poem #97 in this collection, compiled the *Hyakunin Isshu*; I have titled the translation *One Hundred Leaves*. It selects one poem each from one hundred Japanese poets, arranged in loose chronological order, from the 7th century to the 13th century. Teika was a renowned poet and critic of his time and the collection quickly became popular, remaining so to this day, with many children playing a card game version that requires memorization of the verses.

These poems, originally called *waka*, are now commonly called *tanka* and follow a syllable pattern of five lines, 31 syllables, broken into units of 5 / 7 / 5 / 7 / 7. They were generally composed by aristocratic men and women, especially those revolving around the Imperial Court.

Educated nobility were generally expected to compose poems for a variety of social occasions and there were frequent poetry contests at the Imperial Court. Furthermore, unrelated aristocratic men and women could not directly see or speak to each other in open forums during much of this period so they communicated by letters and wooed each other by writing poetry. Since it was the refined upper classes writing poetry, they did not for the most part veer into vulgarity and usually chose to express their feelings and experiences indirectly.

Visual Images

As Japanese writing developed from Chinese characters, which are essentially pictures that convey abstract concepts, it developed a strong visual orientation. *Waka* tend to focus on just one or two images to convey a strong meaning. Emotions and abstract ideas are commonly symbolized through tangible images. This is an example from Kakinomoto no Hitomaro (poem #3):

On a mountain slope
The copper pheasant's tail
Just flows and flows—
So long, like this night
If I'm to sleep alone

The feeling of loneliness is represented by a night that seems long, illustrated by the copper pheasant's long tail.

Pivot Words and Pillow Words

Japanese is full of homonyms, words with different meanings but the same pronunciation. When written in Chinese characters, called *kanji*, the meaning is more easily distinguished, though there are still often different possible meanings. However, when written in the Japanese alphabet system, called *hiragana*, the reader needs to guess among many possibilities.

Japanese poets took advantage of this to introduce extensive wordplay and layers of meaning, writing key words in *hiragana* rather than in the more explicit *kanji*. One example is *shinobu*, which under one reading means a "fern plant," but under another reading means "conceal." So a poet could superficially write about a fern plant pattern on cloth, but actually be talking about his hidden love for somebody. Likewise, *matsu* could mean either "wait" or "pine tree." When writing about pine trees, the poet is likely to be talking about waiting for his lover. In the ancient way of writing "Osaka" in *kanji*, the first character meant "to meet, to rendezvous." Many poets incorporated this double meaning into their poems referencing Osaka.

Pillow words are those that do not necessarily have a literal meaning associated with the theme of the poem, but are a kind of stock phrase that readers of the time would associate with a certain theme. For example, "high sands" is associated with mountain summits and "black hair" is associated with disordered, confused, or tangled feelings.

Nature

Nature is very important in Japanese culture, even to the present day. Part of this relates to the traditional religion of Japan, *Shinto*, in which each element of nature has a deity. Japan is prone to disasters, such as earthquakes, typhoons, and tsunami, so this has left an impression over time on the national psyche.

Almost every poem refers to nature in some way and these references carry additional emotional, allusive, or historical connotation that adds meaning to an otherwise short poem. For example, a deer or monkey crying is a symbol of sadness. The short reeds of Naniwa Bay symbolize short-term trysts since the bay was close to a pleasure district. When poets wrote of the impossibility of a mountain being overrun by the sea, it served as a pledge to love forever.

Season and Time of Day

Like nature, the season and weather have a deep impact on the Japanese psyche and is alluded to in most poems. These seasons have emotional connotation that add a layer of meaning to the poem. For example, autumn is a symbol of loneliness, of the bright and warm part of the year coming to an end. Likewise, an autumn breeze symbolizes sadness. In contrast, spring symbolizes youth, love, and vitality.

Time of day is important too. For example, dusk is a symbol of sadness. Another example is poems that do not mention directly waiting for a missing lover overnight; rather they might mention seeing the morning moon alone.

Overall Experience

Traditionally these poems were chanted slowly when recited. Although it is impossible to get this sense from a book, I have provided the pronunciation for every poem, notes on the literal meaning, the original Japanese in calligraphic font, and art work illustrating each poem's theme.

Everyone's experience of poetry is different, but the way I enjoy these poems is to read them aloud slowly, savoring the sounds, and forming a visual image. Then, while holding that image in mind, I layer in the feelings of the poet and try to imagine the scene, letting it come alive into a moving picture with sounds, scents, and colors.

One Hundred Leaves

百人一首之内
天智天皇

#1 Emperor Tenchi, "Harvest-time in the field"

Translation

By Emperor Tenchi (626-671)

Harvest-time in the field
A hut that's coarsely-thatched,
An autumn refuge—
My sleeves
Are wet with dew.

Original Japanese

天智天皇

秋の田の
かりほの庵の
苫をあらみ
わが衣手は
露にぬれつつ

Pronunciation

Tenchi Tennou

Aki no ta no
Kariho no io no
Toma wo arami
Waga koromode wa
Tsuyu ni nuretsutsu

Literal Notes

Autumn 's field 's
[Hut/harvested-ears-of-grain] 's/of hermitage 's/of
Thatched roof is crude
My sleeve
Of-dew/tears becomes-wet

There are different interpretations of the poem, but mine is that it tells the story of a peasant working the field, taking occasional refuge in a skimpy hut, wiping away the tears from his hard life on his sleeve. Another is that the speaker is all alone in his ramshackle hut in the fields, away from his love, making his sleeves wet with tears.

百人一首之内
持統天皇
一勇斎國芳画

#2 Empress Jitou, "Spring has past"

Translation

By Empress Jitou (645-702)

Spring has past
And summer begun;
The strange, shining
Robes of royals dry—
At Kagu, perfumed mountain of the sky.

Original Japanese	**Pronunciation**
持統天皇	Jitou Tennou
春過ぎて	Haru sugite
夏来にけらし	Natsu kinikerashi
白妙の	Shiro-tae no
衣ほすてふ	Koromo hosu chou
天の香具山	Ama no kagu-yama

Literal Notes

Spring has-past
Summer kicked-off
White [cloth/delicate/mysterious] 's/of
Clothes drying
Heavens's [Kagu/Fragrant-Ingredient] Mountain

Empress Jitou was one of only eight empresses in Japan. In Japan, the imperial line follows male succession, so the empresses were in place only temporarily until a male emperor could take power. This poem symbolically talks about royal succession. In Japanese religion, Kagu is the mountain of a stone door, behind which is the Sun Goddess, who bore the first Japanese emperor. Thus, according to Japanese religion, all Japanese royalty are descended from gods.

In the poem, the speaker sees the summer robes drying and realizes that spring has passed before he knew it. The mention of Mount Kagu, where the royal family comes from, gives it imperial symbolism.

百人一首之内 柿本人丸

#3 Kakinomoto no Hitomaro, “If I’m to sleep alone”

Translation

By Kakinomoto no Hitomaro (662-710)

On a mountain slope
The copper pheasant’s tail
Just flows and flows—
So long, like this night
If I’m to sleep alone

Original Japanese	**Pronunciation**
柿本の人麻呂	Kakinomoto no Hitomaro
あしびきの	Ashi-biki no
山鳥の尾の	Yama-dori no o no
しだり尾の	Shidari-o no
ながながし夜を	Naga-nagashi yo wo
ひとりかも寝む	Hitori kamo nen

Literal Notes

Foot dragging ’s/of
Mountain bird ’s tail ’s
Long hanging tail ’s
Long, long night
Alone maybe sleep?

This tanka says the night will be as long as the long, flowing tail of the copper pheasant if he cannot be with his lover.

百人一首之内
山邊赤人
一勇斎國芳画

#4 Yamabe no Akahito, "White cloth on Fuji's peak"

Translation

By Yamabe no Akahito (700-736)

At Tago Bay,
I'm hit by the sight of
White cloth
On Fuji's peak
And falling snow

Original Japanese	**Pronunciation**
山部赤人	Yamabe no Akahito
田子の浦に	Tago no ura ni
うちいでて見れば	Uchi idete mireba
白妙の	Shiro-tae no
富士の高嶺に	Fuji no taka-ne ni
雪はふりつつ	Yuki wa furitsutsu

Literal Notes

Tago 's Bay at
Hit come out see as
White cloth 's
Fuji 's peak at
Snow falling

百人一首之内 猿丸大夫

#5 Sarumaru no Dayu, "In the mountain's heart"

Translation

By Senior Assistant Minister Sarumaru, Sarumaru no Dayu (active ~ 708-715)

In the mountain's heart
Through crimson leaves
A trampling deer lets out a cry—
A voice that's heard
In autumn sadness

Original Japanese

猿丸大夫

奥山に
紅葉ふみわけ
鳴く鹿の
声きく時ぞ
秋は悲しき

Pronunciation

Sarumaru Dayu

Okuyama ni
Momiji fumiwake
Naku shika no
Koe kiku toki zo
Aki wa kanashiki

Literal Notes

Interior mountain in
Crimson leaves pushing through
Belling deer 's
Voice heard time!
Autumn is sad.

百人一首之内
中納言家持
一勇斎國芳画

#6 Otomo no Yakamochi, "On the Bridge that Magpies Cross"

Translation

By Counselor Yakamochi, Otomo no Yakamochi (718-785)

On the bridge
That magpies cross
The frosty white
Is laid across
As night grows old

Original Japanese	**Pronunciation**
中納言家持	Chuunagon Yakamochi
かささぎの	Kasasagi no
渡せる橋に	Wataseru hashi ni
置く霜の	Oku shimo no
白きを見れば	Shiroki wo mireba
夜ぞふけにける	Yo zo fuke ni keru

Literal Notes

Magpie 's
Crossing bridge on [Could also mean "laying across bridge on"]
Put frost 's
White see can
Night is growing late

A magpie is a black-and-white bird. The bridge that magpies cross could refer to the arc of the skies or heavens (since birds fly across the sky). As they are black-and-white and it is set at night, you can imagine the black-and-white of the Milky Way's arc. Reference to white frost adds to that picture, if you imagine the "milk" of the Milky Way as white frost.

Another level of interpretation is to view "magpies" as a symbol for the people that secretly cross the bridge leading to the palace to meet their lovers, the bridge covered with white frost as the night wore on and time for their trysts ran out. Most likely the poet wrote it with both meanings in mind as this mode of communication between lovers was very common in aristocratic Japan as they exchanged poems.

百人一首之内
安倍仲麻呂
一勇斎國芳

#7 Abe no Nakamaro, “The sky’s meadow above”

Translation

By Abe no Nakamaro (701-770)

I gaze into the distance
And the meadow of sky above
Becomes the Kasuga Shrine
On Mount Mikasa
In the coming moon!

Original Japanese	Pronunciation
安倍仲麿	Abe no Nakamaro
天の原	Ama no hara
ふりさけ見れば	Furisake mireba
春日なる	Kasuga naru
三笠の山に	Mikasa no yama ni
出でし月かも	Ideshi tsuki kamo

Literal Notes

Heaven ’s meadow
Far off see when
Kasuga becomes [Kasuga is a shrine; the characters mean spring day]
Mikasa ’s mountain at
Coming moon

Abe no Nakamaro is said to have written this poem in China at his farewell party before he was to return to Japan. It describes him looking at the vast sky above, seeing the moon, and being reminded of his time in Japan when he visited the Kasuga Shrine to pray for a safe trip to China and saw the same moon. The Kasuga Shrine in classical Japanese literature had the connotation of departure since that is where people went to pray for a safe trip.

Sadly, he was never able to return to Japan; his ship was wrecked. This was the second time he had tried to return to Japan and the second time his ship was wrecked, so he gave up after that and spent the rest of his life in China.

百人一首之内
喜撰法師

#8 Monk Kisen, "My hermit hut"

Translation

By Monk Kisen

My hermit hut
Above the capital,
I live with just a deer—
The world a mountain house
And the people, abandoned.

Original Japanese	**Pronunciation**
喜撰法師	Kisen Houshi
わが庵は 都のたつみ しかぞすむ 世をうぢ山と 人はいふなり	Waga io wa Miyako no tatsumi Shika zo sumu Yo wo uji yama to Hito wa iu nari

Literal Notes

My hermitage
Capital [southeast/stand-watching]
[But/thus/deer] lives
World through [house/inside/within] mountain and
People [say/awe/abandonment/transfer] become

Whether *shika* can be read as a pivot word also meaning "deer" is debatable. Given that there is no *kanji* and the pronunciation is the same as "deer," that is a legitimate reading, but the main meaning is something like "but" or "thus." Still, I liked the possibility of using "deer," so I included it in the translation.

百人一首之内
小野小町
一勇斎國芳画

#9 Ono no Komachi, "The vibrant flower's face has faded"

Translation

By Ono no Komachi (825-900)

The vibrant flower's
Face has faded—
While I gaze in vain
As the world grows old
And the long rain falls

Original Japanese

小野小町

花の色は
うつりにけりな
いたづらに
我が身世にふる
ながめせしまに

Pronunciation

Ono no Komachi

Hana no iro wa
Utsuri ni keri na
Itazura ni
Wa ga mi yo ni furu
Nagame-seshima ni

Literal Notes

Flower 's color
Has faded
While [vainly/surfacely]
My body worldly-life [gets-old/falls]
[Gazing/long-rain]

This poem is layered with double-meaning. In the first line, the flower's color or vibrancy also has romantic or love overtones. The third line can mean in vain or on the surface, meaning either that the author has wasted her life or modifying the next two lines so that on the surface she has grown old and lost her luster, but there is still passion inside. The fourth line refers to herself and says the body and the world has grown old. The fifth line can be read either as gazing or as an abbreviation for long rain. If you take the long rain meaning, it would modify "old" from the fourth line to mean "falling" as in "falling rain."

It has been translated in different ways, some with a natural interpretation of the flower fading, some with an old woman thinking back on the lost beauty of her youth, and some with an old woman having lost her physical beauty but still beautiful inside.

百人一首之内
蝉丸

#10 Semimaru, "Osaka's rendezvous gate"

Translation

By Semimaru

This is the place—
Of comings and goings
And partings of ways;
Of knowing and not knowing too:
Osaka's rendezvous gate.

Original Japanese

蟬丸

これやこの
行くも帰るも
別れては
知るも知らぬも
逢坂の関

Pronunciation

Semimaru

Kore ya kono
Yuku mo kaeru mo
Wakarete wa
Shiru mo shiranu mo
Ousaka no seki

Literal Notes

Of this and this [place]
To go and return also
To part from
To know and know not also
Osaka/rendezvous-hill 's gate

Under this older way of writing "Osaka," it is written as 逢坂, with a different first character than the modern way, written as 大阪. By itself, the Ou in Ousaka is 逢う and pronounced Au, meaning "to meet, rendezvous, tryst, date," thus reinforcing the meaning of the poem.

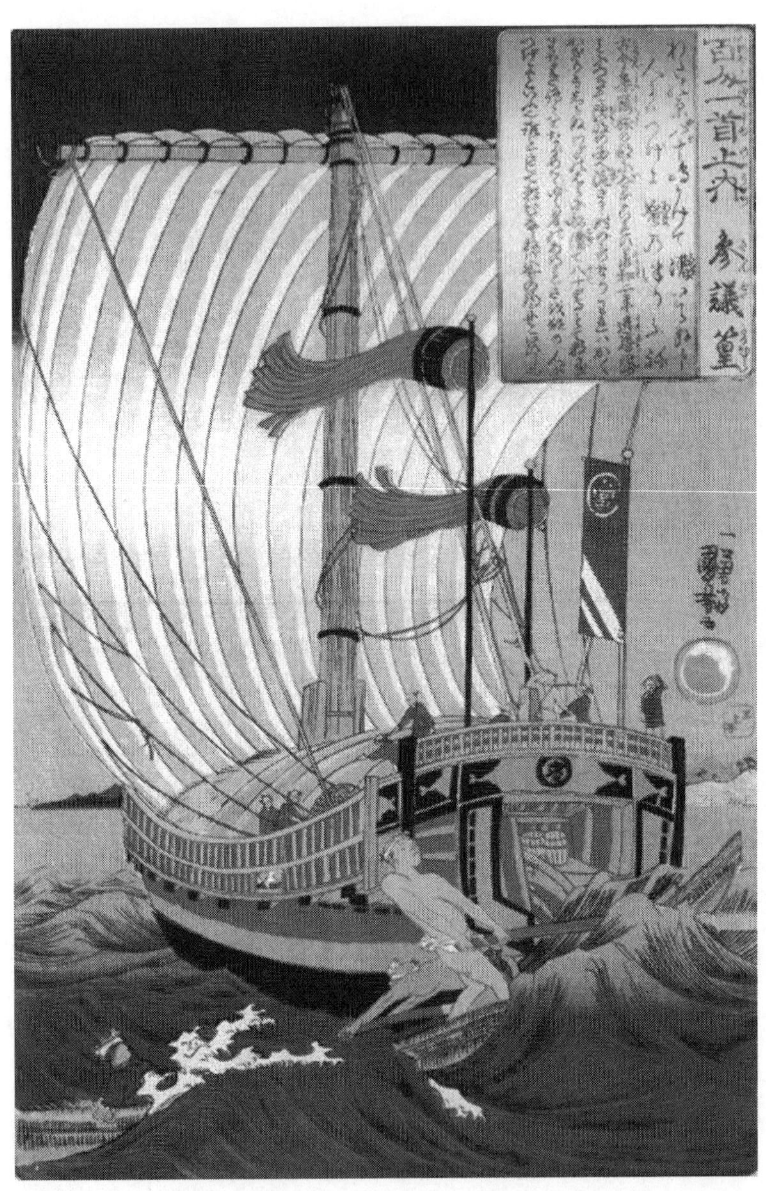
百人一首之内
参議篁

#11 Ono no Takamura, "Tell the people"

Translation

By Counselor Takamura, Ono no Takamura (802-852)

Rowing out
Past Eighty Islands
And the plain of sea—
Tell the people
Of this heaven-tempting boat!

Original Japanese

参議篁

わたの原
八十島かけて
こぎ出ぬと
人には告げよ
あまのつり舟

Pronunciation

Sangi Takamura

Wata no hara
Yasoshima kakete
Kogi idenu to
Hito ni wa tsugeyo
Ama no tsuri bune

Literal Notes

Sea 's meadow
Eighty Islands by way of
Have rowed out and
People inform
Heaven 's tempting boat

Ono no Takamura was a noted poet and state counselor exiled for a year to an island for feigning illness to avoid a mission to China. He wrote this poem upon his exile.

百人一首之内
僧正遍昭
一勇斎國芳画

#12 Monk Henjou, "I see a maiden's form"

Translation

By Monk Henjou (816-890)

Heavenly wind,
The cloud's commute,
Stop your blowing, please—
I see a maiden's form
And want to stay awhile.

Original Japanese

僧正遍昭

天つ風
雲のかよひ路
吹きとぢよ
乙女のすがた
しばしとどめむ

Pronunciation

Soujou Henjou

Ama tsu kaze
Kumo no kayoiji
Fuki toji yo
Otome no sugata
Shibashi todomen

Literal Notes

Heavenly wind
Cloud 's commute route
Blowing close please
Maiden 's appearance
For-a-short-while stay

It is said that Monk Henjou wrote this tanka after seeing young ladies dance at a festival. In the poem, he's referring to Buddhist mythological maidens living in the sky.

百人一首之内
陽成院

#13 Retired Emperor Youzei, “Male and female peaks”

Translation

By Retired Emperor Youzei (869-949)

From Tsukuba’s
Male and female peaks
The Minano River falls
And gathers a pool
Of passion deep

Original Japanese

陽成院

筑波嶺の
峰より落つる
みなの川
恋ぞつもりて
淵となりぬる

Pronunciation

Youzei In

Tsukuba ne no
Mine yori otsuru
Minano gawa
Koi zo tsumorite
Fuchi to nari nuru

Literal Notes

Tsukuba Summit ’s
Peaks from falling
Minano river
Love ! intention and [love is emphasized by the zo particle]
Depths/pool become preceding

When “Minano” is written in *kanji*, its characters are 男女, meaning man-woman, so named because the river’s source is Tsukuba’s twin peaks, which reminded people of a man and a woman.

百人一首之内
河原左大臣

#14 Minamoto no Toru, "Dyed and tangled, trapped in secret love"

Translation

By Minister Kawara, Minamoto no Toru (822-895)

Surrounded by this
Intricate print,
Becoming
Dyed and tangled,
Trapped in secret love.

Original Japanese

河原左大臣

みちのくの
しのぶもぢずり
誰故に
乱れそめにし
我ならなくに

Pronunciation

Kawara no Sadaijin

Michinoku no
Shinobu moji-zuri
Tare yue ni
Midare some ni shi
Ware naranaku ni

Literal Notes

Michinoku 's
[Fern/recollection/forbearance/endure/conceal] cloth printing
Who therefore
[Disordered/confused/disturbed] [to-dye/color/print]
I become

In this *tanka*, the poet sees a fine, intricate fern cloth printing, which reminds him of how tangled and chaotic his feelings are toward the woman he loves. Michinoku was an area that produced cloth used for fern prints and Shinobu was a district in Michinoku. The pronunciation for fern is the same as for remembering or concealing oneself, which gives it a double meaning. In the translation, I am using "surrounded" to capture how the image of the cloth print has taken over his feelings, stirring recollections of his secret love.

百人一首之内
光孝天皇

#15 Emperor Koukou, "While the snow sprinkles on my sleeve"

Translation

By Emperor Koukou (830-887)

I walk the fields
Of spring for you
And pluck the youthful herbs
While snow
Is sprinkling on my sleeve.

Original Japanese	**Pronunciation**
光孝天皇	Koukou Tennou
君がため	Kimi ga tame
春の野に出でて	Haru no no ni idete
若菜つむ	Wakana tsumu
わが衣手に	Waga koromode ni
雪はふりつつ	Yuki wa furi tsutsu

Literal Notes

You on behalf
Spring 's field to-go-out
Young [herbs/greens] [pile-up/pluck/pick-up]
My sleeve on
Snow [falls/sprinkles] while

The word for "you" in this context, 君 or "kimi," is said by a man to a woman with whom he is close. Spring's fields is an archaic way of saying "calm fields of spring."

百人一首之内
中納言行平

#16 Ariwara no Yukihira, "I'll return soon, or die trying"

Translation

By Counselor Yukihira, Ariwara no Yukihira (818-893)

We stand apart
From pines that spring
Along Inaba's peak—
But if I hear your pining song,
I'll come back soon, or die trying.

Original Japanese	**Pronunciation**
中納言行平	Chuunagon Yukihira
立ち別れ	Tachi wakare
いなばの山の	Inaba no yama no
峰に生ふる	Mine ni ouru
まつとしきかば	Matsu to shi kikaba
今かへりこむ	Ima kaeri kon

Literal Notes

Stand parting
[Inaba/leave-if] Mountain 's
[Peak/ridge] [at/to] [grow/spring-up]
[Pine-tree/wait/look-forward/end-of] [year |or| and death/poem] [hear-if]
[Now/soon] [return/go-home] [crowded/to-do-intently]

Almost every line has multiple possible meanings. In this case, the poem describes being away from his lover and uses the image of Mt. Inaba. However, he writes Inaba in *hiragana*, leaving open another reading as "even if I am not there." In the fourth line, "Matsu" can be read as "pine tree" under one *kanji*, but also as "waiting, anticipating, looking forward to" under another *kanji*. "To shi" could either be read together as "year" or separately as "and poem/song" or "and death." So together that line could mean, all equally valid, "if I hear the song of the pines," "if I hear your pining song," "if I hear the years/time of your waiting is like death," among other variations. The last line can be read as "return soon with intention" or "I'll return no matter how crowded the way may be."

百人一首之内 在原業平朝臣

#17 Ariwara no Narihira, "A dye so red"

Translation

By Courtier Ariwara no Narihira (825-880)

Even thousands of years ago,
In the Age of Gods,
No one had heard
Of a dye so red
As the Imperial River

Original Japanese

在原業平朝臣

千早ぶる
神代もきかず
龍田川
からくれないに
水くくるとは

Pronunciation

Ariwara no Narihira Ason

Chihayaburu
Kamiyo mo kikazu
Tatsuta-gawa
Kara kurenai ni
Mizu kukuru to wa

Literal Notes

Thousand years ago
Age-of-Gods also hear not
Tatsuta River [lit. Dragon/imperial-field River]
[Crimson/China/empty/sky] [red/not-give/not-get-dark] about
Water dye as-that

This was composed for a screen painting of autumn leaves in the Tatsuta River. Screen paintings were made with tie-dye; thus the poem refers both to the painting and the scene itself, a river full of bright red autumn leaves.

Traditionally, crimson tears allude to "tears of blood," reflecting scandalous rumors. It was brought to my attention by a reader, Jocelyn Chan, that this poem may have served as a secret note to the Empress Takaiko, regarding a rumored affair with the poet. In this story, the poet recited the poem to her from behind a screen decorated with autumn leaves. While the written version of the poem has the interpretation as above, using different kanji with the same pronunciation can yield the following poem: 血は破るか御世も聞かず竜田川から呉れ無いに見ず潜る永は (Blood rends / What the Emperor cannot hear: / From the Tatsuta River / Comes nothing, / Hidden forever."

百人一首之内
藤原敏行朝臣
朝櫻楼 国芳画

#18 Fujiwara no Toshiyuki, "You hide from greedy eyes"

Translation

By Counselor Fujiwara no Toshiyuki (died in 907)

Approaching the shore
Of Sumiyoshi Bay
While carrying the night, the waves—
And even in this passage of dreams,
You hide from greedy eyes.

Original Japanese	**Pronunciation**
藤原敏行朝臣	Fujiwara no Toshiyuki Ason
住の江の	Sumi no e no
岸による波	Kishi ni yoru nami
よるさへや	Yoru sae ya
夢の通ひ路	Yume no kayoi ji
人目よくらむ	Hito me yoku ran

Literal Notes

Sumi 's Bay 's ["sumi" = to-live/dwell; Sumiyoshi Bay in Osaka, formerly called Naniwa]
Ashore/beach [by-means-of/toward (night/approach)] waves
[Night/approach/is-caused-by/to-depend-on/to-choose] [only/even]
[Dream/vision/illusion] 's [commute/traffic/pass-through] [path/route/road]
[Public-gaze/public-notice/people's-eyes] [nice/frequent/greed/avarice/want] not

This tanka uses extensive word play, the main being "yoru" as a pivot word meaning both "night" and "approaching." In the second line "ni yoru" would usually mean "by means of" but it could also mean "night to" or "approaching to." In the last line, "yoku ran" could mean "hide from," "not often," or "not greedy." The sense of the poem could be either keeping their love a secret (from each other or from people in general), even in dreams, or of his desired lover not accepting his advances, even in dreams. In traditional Japanese symbolism, lovers could communicate with each other in their dreams.

小倉擬百人一首
伊勢
一勇斎國芳画

#19 Lady Ise, "Is that what you mean?"

Translation

By Lady Ise (872-938)

We can never meet again
And even a rendezvous
As short as the reeds
Of Naniwa marshes is too much—
Is that what you mean?

Original Japanese

伊勢

難波潟
みじかき芦の
ふしのまも
あはでこの世を
過ぐしてよとや

Pronunciation

Ise

Naniwa gata
Mijikaki ashi no
Fushi no ma mo
Awade kono yo wo
Sugushite yo to ya

Literal Notes

Naniwa Bay
Short reed 's
[Father-and-son/joint/melody/immortality/lie-down] 's [time/demon/truth] also
[Not-meeting/bubble/foam/froth] this [world/society/age/generation]
[Overdo/go-beyond/too-much] [world/society/more-than/evening] you say ?

小倉
擬百人一首
元良親王

#20 Prince Motoyoshi, "I'm grieving for our scene"

Translation

By Prince Motoyoshi (890-943)

Seeing Naniwa's channel posts,
I'm grieving for our scene,
But now it's all the same:
The troubled waves, we cannot meet again,
For ruin, body and name.

Original Japanese	Pronunciation
元良親王	Motoyoshi Shinnou
わびぬれば	Wabi nureba
今はた同じ	Ima hata onaji
難波なる	Naniwa naru
身をつくしても	Mi wo tsukushite mo
逢はむとぞ思ふ	Awan to zo omou

Literal Notes

[Grieved/pining/simple-beauty/apology] [drama's-love-scene/to-get-wet]
Now [field/close/near/end/tip/point] same
Naniwa become
Body/self [all-sorts-of/all-kinds-of]
Meeting not think

- "Mi wo tsukushite" can means destroy oneself or sacrifice oneself while "mio tsukushi" means "channel marker."
- "Na" in Naniwa is the pronounced the same as the character for "name."
- "Naniwa" is old Osaka and literally means "difficult/impossible waves."

Prince Motoyoshi was known for having a lot of affairs and had one with the wife of retired Emperor Uda. After the story came out, it caused a scandal.

百人一首之内
素性法師

#21 Monk Sosei, "Coming soon"

Translation

By Monk Sosei (died ~ 910)

Just because you said
"Coming soon"
I've hung around waiting
Through the longest night's
Morning moon

Original Japanese	**Pronunciation**
素性法師	Sosei Houshi
今来むと	Ima kon to
いひしばかりに	Iishi bakari ni
長月の	Nagatsuki no
有明の月を	Ariake no tsuki wo
待ち出でつるかな	Machi idetsuru kana

Literal Notes

[Soon/present/immediate] come
[Say/good] [just/merely] because of
Long Month 's
Dawn 's moon
Wait come [hang/suspend] how!

The "Long Month" is the ninth month of the lunar calendar, around October, and is the moon viewing month because it is supposed to show for longer. "Dawn" in this context specifically means dawn after the longest viewing night.

百人一首之内
文屋康秀

#22 Fun'ya no Yasuhide, "'Temper' makes a 'tempest'"

Translation

By Fun'ya no Yasuhide (died ~ 885)

The blowing wind
Uproots and snaps
The autumn grass and trees—
Fitting then that "temper"
Makes a "tempest," as they say.

Original Japanese	**Pronunciation**
文屋康秀	Fun'ya no Yasuhide
吹くからに	Fuku kara ni
秋の草木の	Aki no kusaki no
しをるれば	Shiorureba
むべ山風を	Mube yama kaze wo
あらしといふらむ	Arashi to iuran

Literal Notes

Blow from
Autumn 's grass tree 's [= plants/vegetation]
[See-as/death/branches] [break/snap-off] when
Fitting mountain wind is
[Storm/destruction/lay-waste] so called

This poem puns on the fact that the character for "storm" (嵐) is composed of a mountain (山) on top of wind (風) and is pronounced almost the same as destruction (arasu). Thus it is literally saying that it is fitting that "mountain" + "wind" = "storm" = "destruction."

百人一首之内
大江千里

#23 Ooe no Chisato, "When looking at the moon"

Translation

By Ooe no Chisato (active ~ 883-903)

When looking at the moon
A thousand things
Become sadness—
My autumn alone
Though it is not.

Original Japanese	**Pronunciation**
大江千里	Ooe no Chisato
月見れば	Tsuki mireba
千々に物こそ	Chiji ni mono koso
悲しけれ	Kanashi kere
わが身ひとつの	Waga mi hitotsu no
秋にはあらねど	Aki ni wa aranedo

Literal Notes

Moon see if/when
Thousands into things certainly/[emphasis]
Sad/sorrow become
My self one/even/only 's
Autumn it-is-not although

百人一首之内
菅家

#24 Sugawara no Michizane, "I cannot make an offering"

Translation

By Kan Ke, Sugawara no Michizane (845-903)

On this occasion,
I cannot make an offering:
So I pray that Offering Hill's
Fine brocade of colored leaves
Finds mercy with the gods

Original Japanese	**Pronunciation**
菅家	Kan Ke
このたびは	Kono tabi wa
幣もとりあへず	Nusa mo toriaezu
手向山	Tamukeyama
紅葉のにしき	Momiji no nishiki
神のまにまに	Kami no mani mani

Literal Notes

This occasion
[Type-of-Shinto-offering-staff] [to-take-hands/for-the-time-being] cannot
Temuka Mountain [= Hand-Facing-Mountain]
[Foliage/colored-leaves] 's [brocade/fine-dress]
[God/spirit/divinity] 's at-the-mercy-of

It is said that Kan Ke wrote this after accompanying the retired emperor to Uda's temple at Temuka Mountain (Temuka = Hand Facing = Offering, so Offering Mountain). Protocol demanded that he could not make an offering at the same time as the retired emperor, so he could only offer the mountain's beautiful coat of fall foliage.

小倉擬百人一首
三條右大臣

#25 Fujiwara no Sadakata, "Isn't there some secret way?"

Translation

By Minister Sanjou, Fujiwara no Sadakata (873-932)

Scarlet berries of Mount Osaka—
If it's worthy of the name,
"Rendezvous Hill,"
Isn't there some secret way
For her to come and sleep with me?

Original Japanese

三条右大臣

名にしおはば
逢坂山の
さねかづら
人にしられで
くるよしもがな

Pronunciation

Sanjou Udaijin

Na ni shi owaba
Ousaka-yama no
Sanekazura
Hito ni shirarede
Kuru yoshi mo gana

Literal Notes

[Name-that-it-carries-on-back/be-worthy-of-the-name] if
Osaka/rendezvous-hill Mountain
[Scarlet/come-sleep] kazura
People know not
[Come/reel-in-thread] some-way is-not-there?/I-wish

There is much erotic wordplay and imagery in this one. The old way of writing Osaka was 逢坂 where 逢 by itself is 逢う, pronounced "au," and means "to meet/tryst/rendezvous." Reading 逢坂 as two separate *kanji* rather than as a single word means "rendezvous hill." "Sa ne" by itself means "come, sleep [with me]." Sanekazura is a vine with edible scarlet berries, an erotic image.

小倉擬百人一首
貞信公

#26 Fujiwara no Tadahira, "Autumn-colored maple leaves"

Translation

By Lord Teishin, Fujiwara no Tadahira (880-949)

If Mount Ogura's
Autumn-colored maple leaves
Had heart, they'd wait
Through the deep snow
For a fleeting royal visit

Original Japanese	Pronunciation
貞信公	Teishin Ko
小倉山	Ogurayama
峰のもみじ葉	Mine no momijiba
心あらば	Kokoro araba
今ひとたびの	Ima hitotabi no
みゆきまたなむ	Miyuki matanan

Literal Notes

Ogura Mountain
[Peak/ridge] 's [maple/changing-colors/autumn-color] leaves
Heart/spirit had if
Now [one-time/fleeting/for-a-moment/person-trip] 's
[Imperial-outing-or-visit/deep-snow] wait wish-to

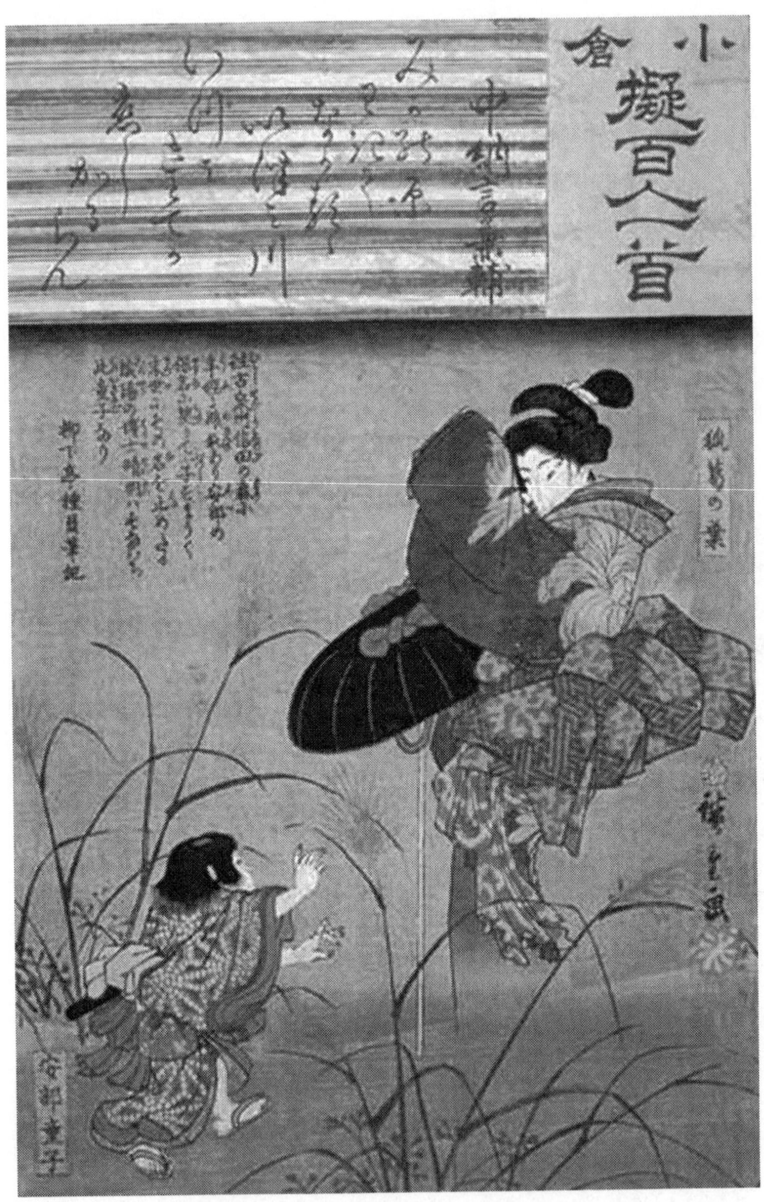
小倉擬百人一首
中納言兼輔
安部童子

#27 Fujiwara no Kanesuke, "Our parting—my yearning"

Translation

By Counselor Kanesuke, Fujiwara no Kanesuke (877-933)

Mika's Meadow, beautiful Mika—
Gushing, foaming,
Izumi River spring:
When did I see you? When abandoned?
Our parting—my yearning

Original Japanese	**Pronunciation**
中納言兼輔	Chuunagon Kanesuke
みかの原	Mika no Hara
わきてながるる	Wakite nagaruru
泉川	Izumi-gawa
いつ見きとてか	Itsu mi kitote ka
恋しかるらむ	Koishi karuran

Literal Notes

[Mika/beautiful+person/smell/join/pleasing/summer] [plain/meadow]
[Gushing/boiling/surging/frothing] while
[Izumi/spring/fountain] river
When [abandon/see] that saying [?/I-wonder]
[Yearned-for/longed-for/missed] [to-cut/drive/spur] [will-be]

小倉擬百人一首
源宗于朝臣

#28 Minamoto no Muneyuki, "All have withered and died"

Translation

By Courtier Minamoto no Muneyuki (died ~ 940)

More desolate than winter,
The lonely mountain hamlet:
Thinking of
The people, the grass—
All have withered and died.

Original Japanese	**Pronunciation**
源宗于朝臣	Minamoto no Muneyuki Ason
山里は	Yama-zato wa
冬ぞさびしさ	Fuyu zo sabishisa
まさりける	Masari keru
人めも草も	Hitome mo kusa mo
かれぬとおもへば	Karenu to omoeba

Literal Notes

Mountain hamlet/village
Winter in loneliness/desolation
Excel/surpass/exceed/outweigh/increase ["keri" emphasizes this]
People eyes/sprouts also grass also
Have withered/died/dried-up/run-out think when

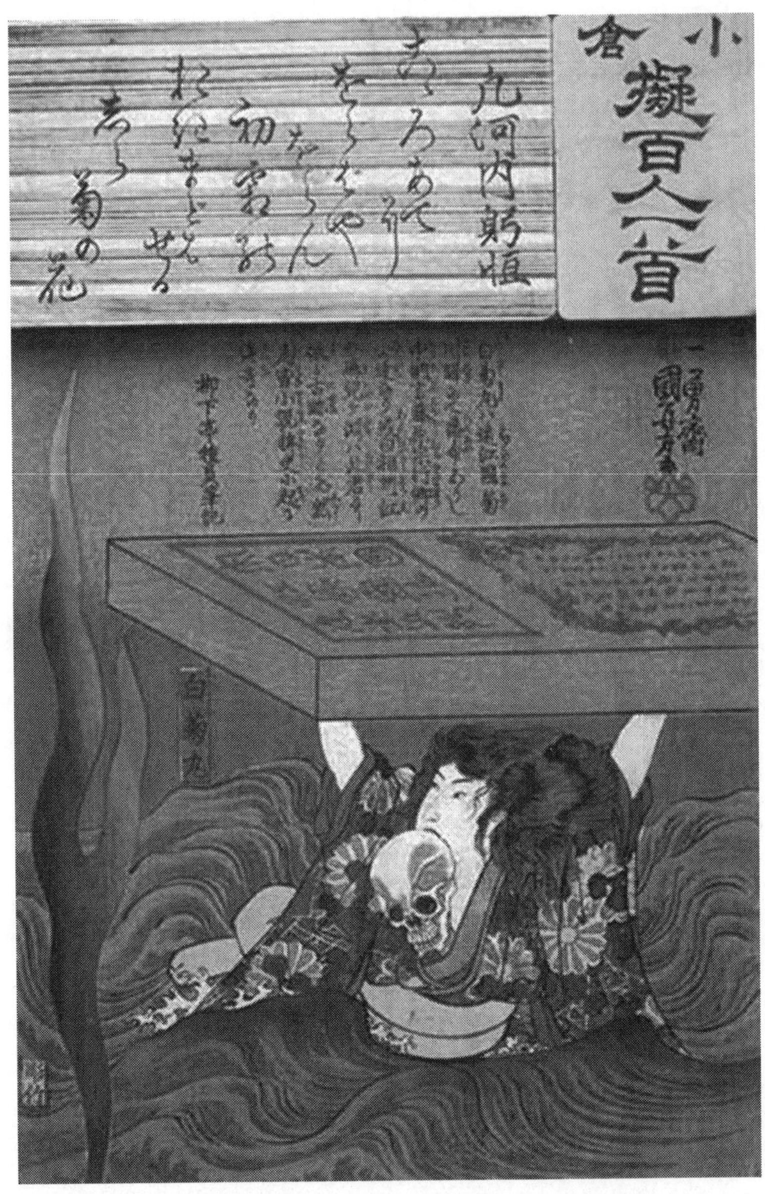
小倉擬百人一首
凡河内躬恒

#29 Oshikochi no Mitsune, "My heart's hit by anticipation"

Translation

Oshikochi no Mitsune (859-925)

My heart's hit by anticipation—
The first frost
Has placed a veil of confusion
Over the white chrysanthemum
And if I pluck it, it will be by chance.

Original Japanese

凡河内躬恒

心あてに
折らばや折らむ
初霜の
おきまどはせる
白菊の花

Pronunciation

Oshikochi no Mitsune

Kokoroate ni
Orabaya oran
Hatsushimo no
Oki madowaseru
Shiragiku no hana

Literal Notes

[Heart-hit/made-up = guess/anticipation] by/with
[Have-chance/opportunity/to-fold] if/when [may-take-it/fold]
First frost 's
[Put/placed/wake/give-up/rise] [window/puzzled/lost/doubts/delusion]
White chrysanthemum flower

In this poem, the speaker wants to pluck a white chrysanthemum flower but cannot find it amid the white snow. White chrysanthemums are the emperor's emblem and they are also the flowers placed on funeral alters.

小倉擬百人一首
壬生忠岑
覚寿
かりや姫

#30 Mibu no Tadamine, "The cold dawn"

Translation

By Mibu no Tadamine (860-920)

Cold dawn,
A waning moon
With no companion—
Since our parting, nothing is so loveless
As the break of day.

Original Japanese	**Pronunciation**
壬生忠岑	Mibu no Tadamine
有明の	Ariake no
つれなくみえし	Tsurenaku mieshi
別れより	Wakare yori
暁ばかり	Akatsuki bakari
うきものはなし	Uki mono wa nashi

Literal Notes

Dawn 's
[Not-take/companionless/cold/heartless] [to-meet/see/get/view]
Parting since
Daybreak nothing but
Love/affection/happy/cheerful thing there is no

The dawn referred to in this poem is usually the period after the 16th day of the lunar month, just after the moon is full, so you can see a setting moon that has become smaller. It was viewed as a cold and heartless symbol. The Japanese does not actually refer to the moon, just to the period of time that people associated with a waning moon.

The second line has no *kanji*, so it can mean multiple things, including "seeing the coldness" or "seeing no companion" or "not taking (me) with." The last line can mean "there is no happiness" or "there is no love."

小倉擬百人一首
坂上是則

#31 Sakanoue no Korenori, "White and mad"

Translation

By Sakanoue no Korenori (died in 930)

At daylight
I gaze at the waning moon
Until the snow is falling
Over Yoshino Village—
White and mad.

Original Japanese

坂上是則

朝ぼらけ
有明の月と
みるまでに
吉野の里に
ふれる白雪

Pronunciation

Sakanoue no Korenori

Asaborake
Ariake no tsuki to
Miru made ni
Yoshino no sato ni
Fureru shirayuki

Literal Notes

Light-of-dawn/daybreak
[Dawn (especially after the 16th day of lunar month)] 's moon and
See/view until
Yoshino 's [country-home/village] at
[Touch/feel/precipitate/to-go-mad] [white-snow]

百人一首之内 春道列樹

#32 Harumichi no Tsuraki, "In a mountain stream"

Translation

By Harumichi no Tsuraki (died in 920)

In a mountain stream
The wind has laid
A river dam,
Blocking the flow
With autumn maple leaves

Original Japanese

春道列樹

山川に
風のかけたる
しがらみは
流れもあへぬ
紅葉なりけり

Pronunciation

Harumichi no Tsuraki

Yama kawa ni
Kaze no kaketaru
Shigarami wa
Nagare mo aenu
Momiji nari keri

Literal Notes

The mountain stream in
Wind 's [laid-along/set-atop]
Wicker-and-bank-barrier [garami also means "about/concerning"]
Flow away cannot
Red-maple-leaves it is only

百人一首之内
紀友則

#33 Ki no Tomonori, "Scattered blossoms"

Translation

By Ki no Tomonori (845-907)

Eternal moon
And fading light—
This spring day,
A restless heart
And scattered blossoms

Original Japanese

紀友則

久方の
光のどけき
春の日に
しづ心なく
花のちるらむ

Pronunciation

Ki no Tomonori

Hisakata no
Hikari nodokeki
Haru no hi ni
Shizu-gokoro naku
Hana no chiruran

Literal Notes

Sky/moon/long-enduring/long-direction
Light remove/take-away/loosen
Spring 's day in
[Quiet/still/lifeless] mind/heart not [= restless/thoughtless/cruel]
Flower 's scatter/revolt/chaos

This poem gives a sense of long-lasting happiness ("the eternal moon") combined with a worry that it is ending ("losing light," "restless heart," "scattered [cherry] blossoms"). Cherry blossoms are known for their vivid beauty, but they only bloom for a couple weeks a year before scattering and disappearing. Some interpretations have this representing unease over whether the peacefulness of the Japanese imperial court would last.

#34 Fujiwara no Okikaze, "Takasago's ancient pines"

Translation

By Fujiwara no Okikaze (active ~ 900-914)

I wonder who
My companion will be
When old friends
And even Takasago's
Ancient pines have disappeared

Original Japanese

藤原興風

誰をかも
知る人にせむ
高砂の
松もむかしの
友ならなくに

Pronunciation

Fujiwara no Okikaze

Tare wo ka mo
Shiru hito ni sen
Takasago no
Matsu mo mukashi no
Tomo nara naku ni

Literal Notes

Who(m) [!/I-wonder]
Known person(s) [do-I-know/do-I-have/to-be]
Takasago 's
Pine also [old-times/nullification/annihilation] 's
Friend(s) disappear

A story from Takasago is of a couple in love that died on the same day and their spirits entered a pine tree, now lodged at the shrine of Takasago. Pine also symbolizes waiting as it has the same pronunciation. In this poem, old friends and even this symbol of long-lasting love (the pine) have disappeared. Thus, this poem can be read as missing a loved one, such as a wife, or of becoming old and seeing your friends die.

Related stories from Takasago: (1) An old couple appearing from the mists of a lake and sitting together talking happily in front of a pine. (2) Two pine trees by the sea, each representing an old man and an old woman in love.

小倉擬百人一首
紀貫之

#35 Ki no Tsurayuki, "Indeed, the hearts of men"

Translation

By Ki no Tsurayuki (866-945)

Indeed, the hearts of men
Cannot be known—
But I can smell the fragrance
Of blossoms long ago
From my native town

Original Japanese

紀貫之

人はいさ
心も知らず
ふるさとは
花ぞむかしの
香に匂ひける

Pronunciation

Ki no Tsurayuki

Hito wa isa
Kokoro mo shirazu
Furusato wa
Hana zo mukashi no
Ka ni nioi keru

Literal Notes

People no/indeed/not-so!
Heart also/equal-to know not
Hometown/native-village
Flower [old-time/nullification/annihilation]
[Incense/smell-with] at [smell/perfume/fragrance] is

Ki no Tsurayuki compiled one of Japan's great classical poetry anthologies, the *Kokinshu*, and contributed about 10% of the poems to the volume. The plum is a symbol of fondness and remembrance of the past. Although not directly written in the poem (just "flower" is written), the introduction in the *Kokinshu* makes clear that it is referring to plum blossoms and was written following a visit to a friend after a long absence.

小倉擬百人一首
清原深養父

#36 Kiyohara no Fukayabu, "Did the moon find its lodging?"

Translation

By Kiyohara no Fukayabu (active ~ 908-930)

On a summer's night
It's evening still,
Yet the dawn appears—
And where among the clouds
Did the moon find its lodging?

Original Japanese

清原深養父

夏の夜は
まだ宵ながら
明けぬるを
雲のいづくに
月やどるらむ

Pronunciation

Kiyohara no Fukayabu

Natsu no yo wa
Mada yoi nagara
Akenuru wo
Kumo no izuku ni
Tsuki yadoruran

Literal Notes

Summer 's night
Yet evening while
Dawns it
Cloud 's where at
Moon rest/lodge

This poem comments on the short summer nights when it feels like dawn appears though it is still evening. The moon disappears during the day, so the speaker wonders rhetorically if it is hiding behind the clouds.

小倉擬百人一首
文屋朝康
玉藻前

#37 Fun'ya no Asayasu, "Scattering ceaselessly"

Translation

By Fun'ya no Asayasu (active ~ 892-902)

Piercing wind blows
Over autumn fields—
The pearls of glistening dew
Come undone,
Scattering ceaselessly.

Original Japanese

文屋朝康

白露を
風のふきしく
秋の野は
つらぬきとめぬ
玉ぞちりける

Pronunciation

Fun'ya no Asayasu

Shiratsuyu wo
Kaze no fukishiku
Aki no no wa
Tsuranuki tomenu
Tama zo chiri keru

Literal Notes

White/glistening dew
Wind 's [blowing/whistling/wiping/laying-a-roof]
Autumn 's/of field
[Go-through/pierce/persist/stick-to] [stop/rest/contain/give-shelter] cannot [alt: a-string-unfixed]
Beads/pearls/ball [geography/dust/dirt/scatter/fall(blossoms, leaves)] does/is/begins

百人一首之内
右近

#38 Lady Ukon, "How I pity your fate"

Translation

By Lady Ukon (active ~ 960-966)

Being forgotten,
I do not worry for myself—
You made a vow
On your mortal life
And how I pity your fate.

Original Japanese	**Pronunciation**
右近	Ukon
忘らるる	Wasuraruru
身をば思はず	Mi wo ba omowazu
誓ひてし	Chikaite shi
人の命の	Hito no inochi no
惜しくもあるかな	Oshiku mo aru kana

Literal Notes

Being forgotten
Body/self for care not
Vow/swear/pledge having-made
Person 's/of [(mortal) life] 's/of
Pitiable/regrettable/disappointing/deserving-better it-is how

In this poem, the narrator speaks of her lover who vowed on his life to be faithful, but has now has abandoned her. Instead of being upset for herself, she fears for his life.

小倉擬百人一首
参議篁

#39 Minamoto no Hitoshi, "Hidden bamboo"

Translation

By Counselor Hitoshi, Minamoto no Hitoshi (880-951)

Hidden bamboo
Among a field of reeds—
Though I've concealed myself so far,
I wonder if my love for you
Is too much to hide.

Original Japanese

参議等

浅茅生の
小野の篠原
忍ぶれど
あまりてなどか
人の恋しき

Pronunciation

Sangi Hitoshi

Asajiu no
Ono no shinohara
Shinoburedo
Amarite nado ka
Hito no koishiki

Literal Notes

[(Broad field of sparsely growing, coarse, thick grass) or
shallow/superficial/shameful/wretched reed life/birth] 's/of
Plain/field 's/of bamboo-grass meadow
[Conceal-oneself/hide] though
[Not-very/not-much/too-much] why/etc. ?
Person 's [love/yearn-for/miss]

In the pronunciation, there is a pun between *shino*hara (*bamboo* meadow) and *shino*buredo (*conceal* though). The poet is comparing his hidden love to bamboo hiding in a field of thick reeds, but his love is so much that he may not be able to continue hiding it.

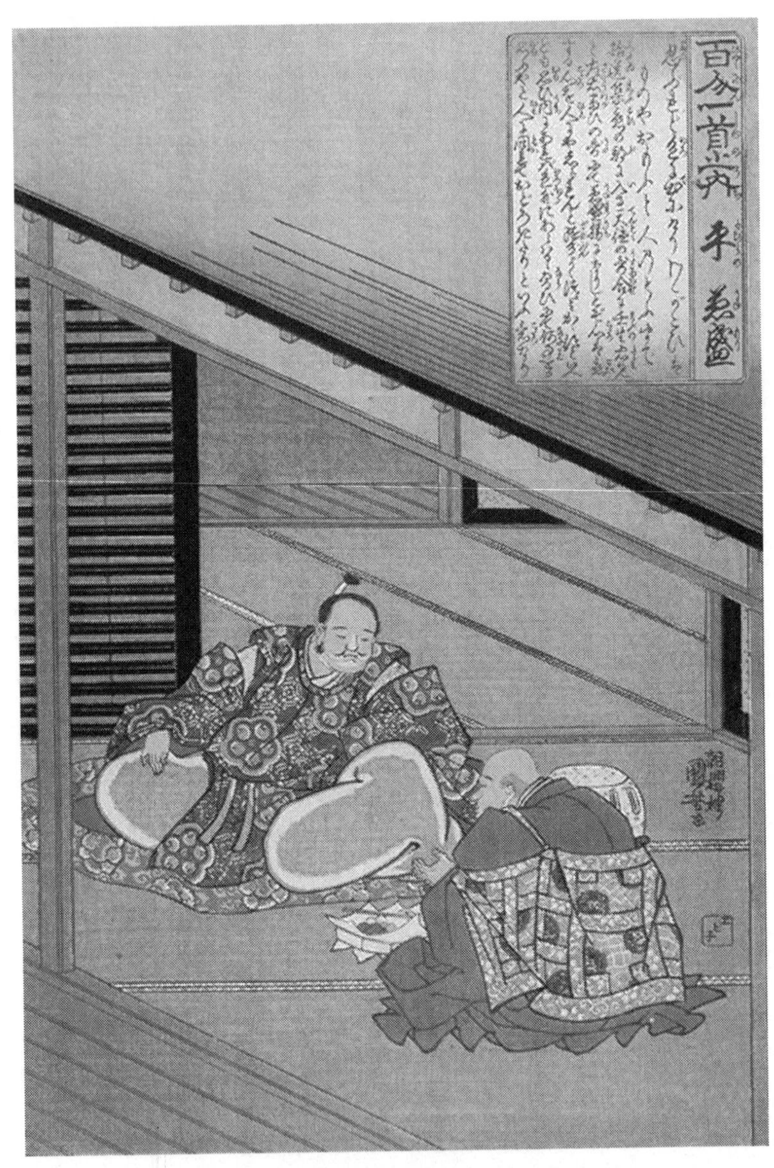
百人一首之内
平兼盛

#40 Taira no Kanemori, "Is something on your mind?"

Translation

By Taira no Kanemori (died in 991)

Though I've concealed it,
My color has shown
A yearning passion—
So she asked,
"Is something on your mind?"

Original Japanese	**Pronunciation**
平兼盛	Taira no Kanemori
忍ぶれど	Shinoburedo
色に出でにけり	Iro ni ide ni keri
わが恋は	Waga koi wa
物や思ふと	Mono ya omou to
人の問ふまで	Hito no tou made

Literal Notes

[Hidden/concealed-myself] though
[Color/love/love-affair/lover] [has-gone-out]
[My/harmony/peace] [love/tender-passion/yearning]
[Thing/object/substance/something] [feeling/thinking]
Person 's question [until/as-far-as/so-much-so]

This poem was an entrant in a poetry contest and was tied for first place. The emperor broke the tie by favoring this one.

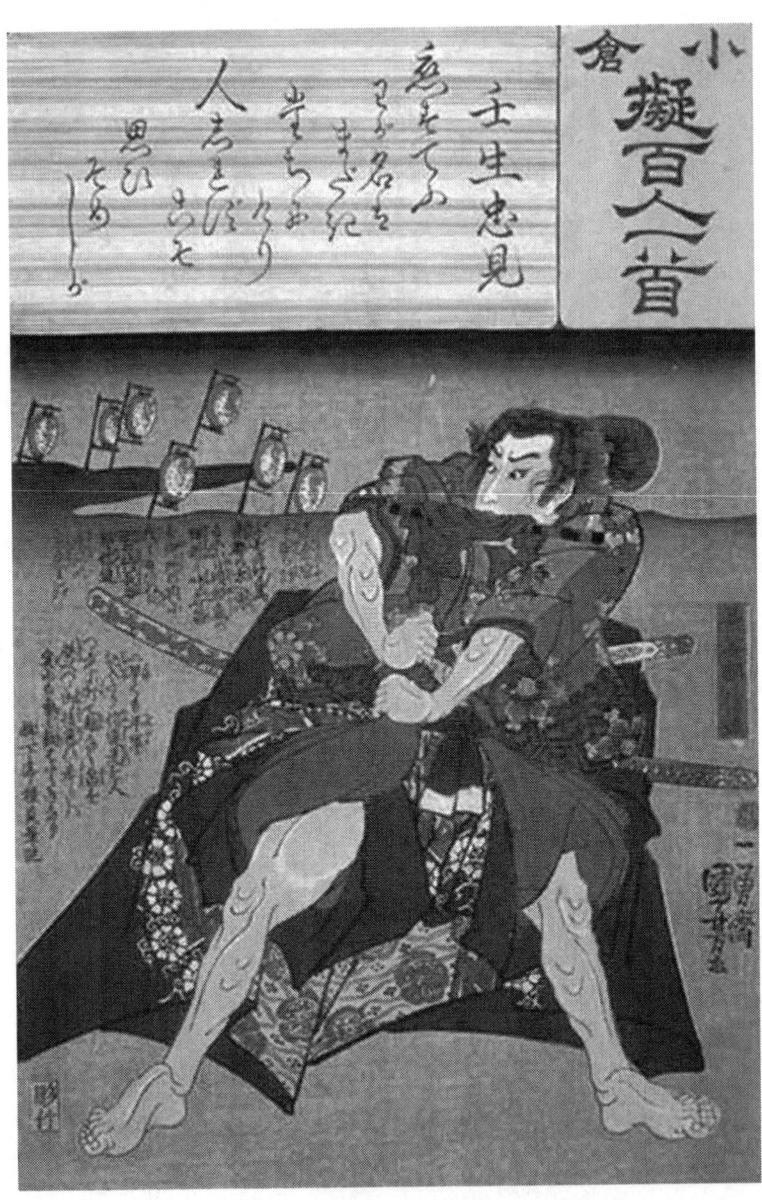
小倉
擬百人一首
壬生忠見

#41 Mibu no Tadami, "The secret... they could not know!"

Translation

By Mibu no Tadami (active ~ 954-960)

They're saying I've fallen in love
And the rumor's already out—
I'm in this situation now,
But the secret... they could not know!
So how did my feelings show?

Original Japanese	**Pronunciation**
壬生忠見	Mibu no Tadami
恋すてふ	Koisu chou
我が名はまだき	Waga na wa madaki
立ちにけり	Tachi ni keri
人しれずこそ	Hito shirezu koso
思ひそめしか	Omoi someshi ka

Literal Notes

[Love(to do) = to-fall-in-love/to-love] saying
My name/reputation [still/as-yet/already/before-daylight]
[To-find-oneself(in a situation)/depart] has
[People-know-cannot = secretly] !
Thought/felt [beginning/dyeing/coloring] ?

百人一首之内 清原元輔

#42 Kiyohara no Motosuke, "You have made a pledge"

Translation

By Kiyohara no Motosuke (908-990)

You have made a pledge
On your sleeves, leaving mementos
Wrung dry repeatedly—
Yet the waves overran
The Endless Mountain Pine.

Original Japanese	**Pronunciation**
清原元輔	Kiyohara no Motosuke
ちぎりきな	Chigiriki na
かたみに袖を	Katami ni sode wo
しぼりつつ	Shibori tsutsu
末の松山	Sue no Matsuyama
波こさじとは	Nami kosaji to wa

Literal Notes

[Pledge/promise/swear/have-sex/tear-up/do-vigorously] have !
[Mutually/shoulders/one-side-of-body/memento/souvenir] sleeves that
[Press/wring/squeeze] [while/repeatedly]
Sue 's pine mountain [sue = place name, or "end"]
Waves [shall-cross-over] it-was-said

This poem had a note saying it was written for someone whose lover changed her mind. It also refers to sleeves wrung dry (from tears). "Sue no" means "to the end" and "pine" is a symbol for waiting because it has the same pronunciation as the character meaning "to wait." So the mountain's name means to "wait until the end." It refers to a poem in the classical Japanese poetry anthology, *Kokinshu*, poem #1093, with the line that they will love each other until the waves overrun Suenomatsu, a mountain in northern Japan.

You kindle my heart	君をおきて	Kimi wo okite
And I will hold the flame	あだし心を	Adashi kokoro wo
Until the end—	わが持たば	Waga mota ba
When the waves	末の松山	Sue no Matsuyama
Cross the Endless Mountain Pine!	浪もこえなむ	Nami mo koenamu

百人一首之内
権中納言敦忠

#43 Fujiwara no Atsutada, "It is as if I hadn't loved"

Translation

Counselor Atsutada, Fujiwara no Atsutada (906-943)

When I compare
My heart since
Our rendezvous
To what it was before—
It is as if I hadn't loved.

Original Japanese

権中納言敦忠

逢ひ見ての
後の心に
くらぶれば
むかしは物を
思はざりけり

Pronunciation

Gon Chuunagon Atsutada

Ai mite no
Nochi no kokoro ni
Kurabureba
Mukashi wa mono wo
Omowazari keri

Literal Notes

[Meet/date/tryst/rendezvous] [see/hope/try] 's/of
[Later/afterwards/since/future] 's/of heart to
[Compare/compete/vie] when
[Old-time] thing
Feeling not had

百人一首之内
中納言朝忠

#44 Fujiwara no Asatada, "If our rendezvous..."

Translation

Counselor Asatada, Fujiwara no Asatada (910-967)

If our rendezvous
Were to cease,
By no means
Would I carry hatred—
For her or for myself

Original Japanese

中納言朝忠

逢ふことの
絶えてしなくば
中々に
人をも身をも
恨みざらまし

Pronunciation

Chuunagon Asatada

Au koto no
Taete shi naku ba
Nakanaka ni
Hito wo mo mi wo mo
Urami zaramashi

Literal Notes

[Meetings/rendezvous] 's
[Stopped/discontinued/cut-off] nothing if
[Very/considerably/by-no-means]
Person/her-and-body/self also
[Resent/blame/curse/bear-a-grudge] not would

小倉擬百人一首
謙徳公
八百屋お七

#45 Fujiwara no Koremasa, "By my own folly"

Translation

Official Kentoku, Fujiwara no Koremasa (924-972)

I do not think
A friend will meet me
With compassion—
By my own folly
I will die unloved

Original Japanese	**Pronunciation**
謙徳公	Kentoku Ko
あはれとも	Aware to mo
いふべき人は	Iu beki hito wa
思ほえで	Omooede
身のいたづらに	Mi no itazura ni
なりぬべきかな	Narinu beki kana

Literal Notes

[To-meet/come-together/pity/sorrow/grief/compassion] [also/friend]
[To-say/call] [must/out/should] person
Thinking/feeling/believing not
Body/self 's/of prank/trick/joke/folly/mischief
Become not must how/alas!

"Itazura ni naru" = to die of love

小倉擬百人一首
曾祢好忠

#46 Sone no Yoshitada, "Direction unknown"

Translation

Sone no Yoshitada (active ~ 985)

As a sailor crossing
The Yura strait
With rudder broken:
Love's path—fire and ash—
Direction unknown

Original Japanese

曾禰好忠

由良のとを
わたる舟人
かぢをたえ
行くへもしらぬ
恋の道かな

Pronunciation

Sone no Yoshitada

Yura no to wo
Wataru funabito
Kaji wo tae
Yukue mo shiranu
Koi no michi kana

Literal Notes

[Wherefore good = Yura strait] 's and [doing]
[Cross-over/go-across] [sailor/boatman/passenger]
[Rudder/helm/fire] [die-out/peter-out/go-extinct/bear/endure]
[Going direction = whereabouts/course/direction] [also] [know-not]
Love 's path how!

小倉擬百人一首
恵慶法師

#47 Monk Egyo, “The vines and weeds”

Translation

Monk Egyo (active ~ 962-986)

The vines and weeds
Entangle this cottage
Alone
And no one saw
The coming autumn

Original Japanese

恵慶法師

八重むぐら
しげれる宿の
さびしきに
人こそ見えね
秋は来にけり

Pronunciation

Egyo Houshi

Yae-mugura
Shigereru yado no
Sabishiki ni
Hito koso miene
Aki wa ki ni keri

Literal Notes

[Multi-layered/doubled] [creepers/trailing-plants]
[Grow-thickly/be-in-full-leaf/rampant/luxuriate] [shelter/lodging/cottage] ’s
Lonely/loneliness/missing-someone
People this see cannot
Autumn has come

百人一首之内
源重之

#48 Minamoto no Shigeyuki, “Rocks engulfed”

Translation

Minamoto no Shigeyuki (died ~ 1000)

Rocks engulfed
And wracked by waves
Then smashed to pieces—
An aching wind,
A time recalled.

Original Japanese	**Pronunciation**
源重之	Minamoto no Shigeyuki
風をいたみ	Kaze wo itami
岩うつ波の	Iwa utsu nami no
おのれのみ	Onore nomi
くだけて物を	Kudakete mono wo
おもふ頃かな	Omou koro kana

Literal Notes

Wind/breeze [does] [pain/ache/grief/hurt/damage/mourning/lamenting]
Rock/crag [hit/attack/depression/low-spirits] wave ’s
[Oneself/you (insulting)] [drink/engulf/suppress/make-light-of/conceal]
[Break-into-pieces/smash/to-be-worried] [things/her] [does]
[Think/feel/desire/recall] time/about how!

#49 Oonakatomi no Yoshinoubu, "By the Royal Gate"

Translation

Courtier Oonakatomi no Yoshinoubu (921-991)

By the Royal Gate
The guards' fire
Burns by night and
Blows out by day:
I think of you

Original Japanese	**Pronunciation**
大中臣能宣朝臣	Oonakatomi no Yoshinoubu Ason
みかき守	Mikakimori
衛士のたく火の	Eji no taku hi no
夜はもえ	Yoru wa moe
昼は消えつつ	Hiru wa kie tsutsu
物をこそおもへ	Mono wo koso omoe

Literal Notes

Imperial Palace gates
Guard 's kindled fire 's
Night by burning
Day by [extinguished/overcome-by-grief]
Things to indeed think

The poet is comparing the passion of him and his lover to the Palace Guard's fire, which only burns at night.

小倉擬百人一首
藤原義孝

#50 Fujiwara no Yoshitaka, "For your sake"

Translation

Fujiwara no Yoshitaka (954-974)

For your sake
I valued
Not even my life—
But how I've come
To desire it long

Original Japanese	**Pronunciation**
藤原義孝	Fujiwara no Yoshitaka
君がため	Kimi ga tame
惜しからざりし	Oshi kara zarishi
命さへ	Inochi sae
ながくもがなと	Nagaku mo gana to
おもひけるかな	Omoi keru kana

Literal Notes

You for-sake/on-behalf
[Regrettable/disappointing/precious/dear/almost-but-not] from [was-not]
(Mortal) life even
Lengthy also [would-be-nice]
Thought/feel have how!

小倉擬百人一首
藤原實方朝臣

#51 Fujiwara no Sanekata, "Etched by fire and drawn to skin"

Translation

By Courtier Fujiwara no Sanekata (died in 999)

How little you know
Of the burning jolt I feel—
As moxa grass
That's etched by fire
And drawn to skin

Original Japanese

藤原実方朝臣

かくとだに
えやはいぶきの
さしも草
さしも知らじな
もゆる思ひを

Pronunciation

Fujiwara no Sanekata Ason

Kaku to dani
E-ya-wa i-buki no
Sashi-mogusa
Sashimo shiraji na
Moyuru omoi wo

Literal Notes

[Each/every/respectively/write/draw/scratch] [even/at-least]
[Draw/paint/get/and-how] [(Tell-could)/Mt.-Ibuki/Juniper-tree/breath(e)]
[To-point/select/shine/tinged-with/plant/as-the] [mugwort/moxa-grass]
[To-point/select/etc.] [not-having/unaffected-by/aside/know-not (about)]
[Burning/(also+shake/rock/jolt)] [feeling+fire(if "hi" is by itself)]

Every line has a lot of wordplay, making it nearly impossible to translate. "Buki" can be read as a form of "beki," meaning "could" or "should." In that case, "i" in "i-buki" would be "to tell/say" so it would mean "how could I say/tell." But "Ibuki" is also the name of a mountain with purple-colored flowers, a Juniper tree that's fiery red/orange in autumn, and also means "to breathe" or "breath." It is a prime example of the multi-faceted wordplay possible in Japanese.

There is also the repetition of "sashimo." "Sashi-mogusa" is a type of grass that was burned into the skin for medicinal purposes. Separately, "sashi" means a variety of things, listed above.

小倉擬百人一首
藤原道信朝臣

#52 Fujiwara no Michinobu, "I curse the light of day"

Translation

By Courtier Fujiwara no Michinobu (972-994)

It's dawn and though I know
The night's love scene
Will play again—
I still curse
The light of day

Original Japanese	**Pronunciation**
藤原道信朝臣	Fujiwara no Michinobu Ason
明けぬれば	Akenureba
暮るるものとは	Kururu mono to wa
知りながら	Shiri nagara
なをうらめしき	Nao urameshiki
あさぼらけかな	Asaborake kana

Literal Notes

[To-dawn/grow-light/open] [wet/paint when -- or "love-scene"]
[Sunset/dusk/grow-dark/close] is thing [that]
[Know/understand/feel] [though/while/even-though]
[Furthermore/nevertheless/mischief/common] [resent/curse/blame/regret]
[Light-of-dawn/daybreak] how!/alas!

The poem originally had a note saying it was sent to a woman after returning home on a snowy day.

百人一首之内

#53 Mother of Michitsuna, "Do you know that feeling?"

Translation

By the Mother of Right Imperial Guard Michitsuna (~937-995)

Sighing continuously
I find myself sleeping
In an empty room
Through the long dawn—
Do you know that feeling?

Original Japanese	**Pronunciation**
右大将道綱母	Udaisho Michitsuna no Haha
なげきつつ	Nageki tsutsu
ひとりぬる夜の	Hitori nuru yo no
明くる間は	Akuru ma wa
いかに久しき	Ikani hisashiki
ものとかは知る	Mono to ka wa shiru

Literal Notes

[Sigh/lament/grieve] [-ing/while/doing-continuously]
Alone [found (myself)/sleep] night 's
[Open/daylight/empty] [comes] [period-of-time/until/room]
[How/aforementioned/threaten/menace] [Long-time (since the last time)]
Thing/that [for-example] know?

The author was famous for her poetry and beauty. It is said she wrote this in reply to her husband, who scolded her for taking a long time to open the door after he came to her late at night during one of his rare visits (aristocratic married couples lived apart at the time and the man visited his wife when he wanted to spend the night). "Akura ma" can be read both as "until daylight comes" or as "empty room."

小倉擬百人一首
儀同三司母
男山一駄
関取江
一勝男節一連
稲川丈江

#54 Mother of Gido Sanshi, "If it's my fate"

Translation

By the Mother of Gido Sanshi (died in 996)

If it's my fate
That you will find it hard
To remember me,
I wish my life
Restricted to today.

Original Japanese	**Pronunciation**
儀同三司母	Gido Sanshi no Haha
忘れじの	Wasureji no
行末までは	Yukusue made wa
難ければ	Katakereba
今日を限りの	Kyou wo kagiri no
命ともがな	Inochi to mo gana

Literal Notes

[Forget/leave-carelessly] not 's/of
[Fate/one's-future] until/into
Difficult if
Today [restrict/limit/confine]
[Mortal-life] [I-wish]

In the last line, "to mo" can be read as "tomo" as in "friend," "to mo" as in "even so" or together with the ending "to mogana" as in "this is what I wish."

小倉擬百人一首
大納言公任

#55 Fujiwara no Kintou, “The waterfall’s sound”

Translation

By Chief Counselor Kintou, Fujiwara no Kintou (966-1041)

A waterfall’s sound:
And though it died
But long ago,
Its name still flows,
Continuing to be heard.

Original Japanese	**Pronunciation**
大納言公任	Dainagon Kintou
滝の音は	Taki no oto wa
絶えて久しく	Taete hisashiku
なりぬれど	Narinuredo
名こそ流れて	Na koso nagarete
なほ聞えけれ	Nao kikoe kere

Literal Notes

Waterfall/rapids ’s sound/noise
[Petering/dying-out/ceasing/stopping] [long-time]
Becomes not though
Name/reputation [the-more-so] [flowing/running/washed-away]
Still/moreso hear can

This tanka is about a waterfall constructed for a previous emperor that was very famous because of stories, but had since dried up. A previous version of the poem used “ito” instead of “oto,” making it the “waterfall’s thread” instead of the “waterfall’s sound.”

百人一首之内
和泉式部
一勇斎国芳画

#56 Lady Izumi Shikibu, "All will be a memory"

Translation

By Lady Izumi Shikibu (976? – 1020)

Soon, we will not be
In this world together
And all will be a memory:
Now, for just a moment,
How I wish to meet.

Original Japanese

和泉式部

あらざらむ
この世の外の
思ひ出に
今ひとたびの
逢ふこともがな

Pronunciation

Izumi Shikibu

Arazaran
Kono yo no hoka no
Omoide ni
Ima hitotabi no
Au koto mo gana

Literal Notes

Be soon probably not
[This-world/this-present-life] 's/of [another-place/outside-of] 's/of
Recall/remember to
Now [for-a-moment/one-time/person-trip]
Meeting [I-wish or friend+how!]

The notes to the poem say it was sent to someone very ill. We do not know if it was a friend or a lover.

小倉擬百人一首
紫式部

#57 Lady Murasaki Shikibu, "A chance encounter"

Translation

By Lady Murasaki Shikibu (~ 973-1014)

A chance encounter,
Seeing a vanished friend—
Or was it?
The cloud-covered
Midnight moon

Original Japanese	**Pronunciation**
紫式部	Murasaki Shikibu
めぐりあひて	Meguri aite
見しやそれとも	Mishi ya sore to mo
わかぬ間に	Wakanu ma ni
雲がくれにし	Kumo-gakure ni shi
夜半の月かげ	Yowa no tsuki kage

Literal Notes

[Around/concerning/pass-a-time] [companion/partner/lose-interest/tire-of]
[See-have] [or/or-else/either... or.../if-it-were/that-friend]
Understand [not-time-period/so-or-not]
[Disappear/vanish/go-away]
[Midnight/middle-of-night] 's moon light

Lady Murasaki Shikibu was the author of the classic story, *Tale of Genji.* The note to the poem says it was written after seeing a childhood friend at night. "Sore to mo" as "soretomo" can be read as "or" or "if it were," but if "sore tomo," it means "that friend." Although the most common meaning of "meguri aite" would be something like "we met," "around when we met," or "we met by chance," individually, the words could mean "passing time" and "losing interest." Some sources, including Fujiwara no Teika's original *Hyakunin Isshu* compilation, have the last word as "kana," an exclamation, instead of "kage," meaning light or shadow; however, the original is written as "kage" and this seems to be the more interesting choice in the editor's opinion.

小倉擬百人一首
大貳三位
妻浅香
應需 豊國画
横山太郎

#58 Lady Kataiko, "I am the rustling stalks"

Translation

By Daini no Sanmi, Lady Kataiko (~ 999-1082)

As Mount Arima
Sends the winds
Over Ina's bamboo fields—
I am the rustling stalks,
So how could I forget you?

Original Japanese	**Pronunciation**
大弐三位	Daini no Sanmi
ありま山	Arimayama
猪名の笹原	Ina no sasawara
風吹けば	Kaze fukeba
いでそよ人を	Ide soyo hito wo
忘れやはする	Wasure ya wa suru

Literal Notes

Arima Mountain
Ina 's bamboo-grass fields
Wind blows when/as
Well/indeed [being-like/this/rustling-of-leaves] person/man
Forget [ironic/rhetorical-question] do

Daini no Sanmi is the daughter of Lady Murasaki Shikibu. It is said that this was sent in reply to a lover's letter complaining that he had not heard from her.

小倉擬百人一首

#59 Lady Akazome Emon, "I waited but should've slept"

Translation

By Lady Akazome Emon (956-1041)

I waited
But should've slept—
Alas, the night grew late,
And I saw
The setting moon

Original Japanese	**Pronunciation**
赤染衛門	Akazome Emon
やすらはで	Yasurawade
寝なまし物を	Nenamashi mono wo
小夜更けて	Sayo fukete
かたぶくまでの	Katabuku made no
月を見しかな	Tsuki wo mishi kana

Literal Notes

[Waiting (and being disappointed)/hesitation]
Sleep better thing
Evening [getting-late]
Decline until
Moon see how!/alas!

The author wrote this on behalf of her sister when her sister's husband did not visit as expected.

百人一首之内
小式部内侍

#60 Lady Koshikibu no Naishi, "Unseen"

Translation

By Lady Koshikibu no Naishi (999-1025)

Far away—
From Mount Oe
To Ikuno Road
And Heaven's Bridge:
Unseen

Original Japanese	**Pronunciation**
小式部内侍	Koshikibu no Naishi
大江山	Oeyama
いく野の道の	Ikuno no michi no
とほければ	To kereba
まだふみも見ず	Mada fumi mo mizu
天の橋立	Ama no Hashidate

Literal Notes

Oe Mountain
[(Go-field/plain)/Ikuno] 's road 's
Far/reject if/while
[As-yet/not-yet] [letter/writings/step-on/experience/distaste] see not
Heaven 's bridge standing/rising

The main pivot word here is "fumi," which could either mean "trod on" or "letter." So you could equally read the line as "I have not seen a letter" or "I have not trod on and seen..." Mount Oe, Ikuno Road, and "Heaven's Bridge" are all landmarks along the way to Tango Bay, arranged in geographical order.

Lady Koshikibu is the daughter of Izumi Shikibu (#56), a famous poet. People suspected her mother was helping her write poetry, so one day when her parents were vacationing at Tango Bay, she was selected for a poetry contest. According to the story, one of the male poets, Sadayori (#64), stopped her and suggested she must be anxiously awaiting a letter from her mother. At that, she is said to have made up this tanka on the spot. Sadayori, unable to respond in kind, walked away. After that, her fame as a poet increased rapidly.

百人一首之内 伊勢大輔

#61 Lady Ise no Osuke, "From the ancient capital of Nara"

Translation

By Lady Ise no Osuke (~ 989-1060)

From the ancient
Capital of Nara—
An eight-fold cherry tree
Now scents
Our Nine-Fold Palace

Original Japanese	**Pronunciation**
伊勢大輔	Ise no Osuke
いにしへの	Inishie no
奈良の都の	Nara no miyako no
八重桜	Yae-zakura
今日九重に	Kyou kokonoe ni
匂ひぬるかな	Nioi nuru kana

Literal Notes

Antiquity/ancient time 's
Nara 's metropolitan/capital 's
Eight-fold cherry-tree
Today [ninefold/imperial-palace]
[Odor/scent/smacks-of] [arises/ends-up] how!/alas!

The Emperor ordered this poem written to commemorate a gift of eight-fold cherry trees from Nara. Nara was the former capital of Japan, which later changed to Kyoto. The Imperial Palace was called the nine-fold palace because of its nine walls.

小倉擬百人一首
清少納言

#62 Lady Sei Shounagon, "The rendezvous gate will not open"

Translation

By Lady Sei Shounagon (~ 966-1017)

Late into the night
A cock's mimicked cry
Attempts to deceive a friend:
But the rendezvous gate
Will not open

Original Japanese	Pronunciation
清少納言	Sei Shounagon
夜をこめて	Yo wo komete
鳥の空音は	Tori no sorane wa
はかるとも	Hakaru tomo
よにあふさかの	Yo ni Ausaka no
関はゆるさじ	Seki wa yurusaji

Literal Notes

Night [crowded/packed/go-into/do-intently/advanced]
Cock 's [imitated-crow/lie]
[Plot/attempt/plan/deceive] [friend/and/though]
[Night/world] [Osaka/rendezvous-hill] 's
[Gate/barrier] [loosen/shake/allow] not

Lady Sei Shounagon is also the author of the classic *Pillow Book.* This poem makes reference to a Chinese story where a prince was held captive in hostile territory. He and his retainers managed to escape in the middle of the night. When approaching the barrier gate, one of his retainers imitated a cock's cry so well that the real cocks began to cry out also. The guards, being fooled by the cries into thinking that morning was beginning, threw open the gates, allowing the prince and his retainers to escape.

This allusion is said to be a reply to the poet's lover when he left in the middle of the night, claiming that he heard the cocks crowing and so could not be seen while his master, the Emperor, was in seclusion. Also of note is that the pronunciation for Osaka's gate at that time was the same as that for "rendezvous hill gate."

百人一首之内
左京大夫道雅

#63 Fujiwara no Michimasa, "Now that my love must die"

Translation

By Head Magistrate of the Left Michimasa, Fujiwara no Michimasa (992-1054)

Now that
Our love must die
I only wish
I could tell you
Without a messenger

Original Japanese	Pronunciation
左京大夫道雅	Sakyou no Daibu Michimasa
今はただ	Ima wa tada
思ひ絶えなむ	Omoi taenan
とばかりを	To bakari wo
人づてならで	Hito-zute nara de
いふよしもがな	Iu yoshi mo gana

Literal Notes

Now just/that
[Feeling/thoughts] [die-out/peter-out/become-extinct/cease]
Just/only this
[Message/hearsay] without
Say means/reason [I-wish/want]

The poet had fallen in love with Princess Masako and was seeing her secretly. However, she was in charge of the shrine of Ise and therefore supposed to be celibate. Once the Emperor found out, he put the princess under female guardians and the poet was not allowed to see her anymore. He wrote her that he accepted the Emperor's decision and had to cut off his love, but wished he could tell her this in person rather than through a messenger.

思ひ絶えなむ (Omoi taenan) can mean either "feelings die out" or "to die of love."

百人一首之内
権中納言定頼

#64 Fujiwara no Sadayori, "On the light of dawn"

Translation

By Counselor Sadayori, Fujiwara no Sadayori (995-1045)

On the light of dawn,
Faintly, slowly
Through fog and mist
From Uji River—
The fishing stakes appear

Original Japanese

権中納言定頼

朝ぼらけ
宇治の川ぎり
たえだえに
あらはれわたる
ぜぜの網代木

Pronunciation

Gon Chuunagon Sadayori

Asaborake
Uji no kawagiri
Tae-dae ni
Araware wataru
Zeze no ajirogi

Literal Notes

[Light-of-dawn/daybreak]
Uji 's river [fog/mist/spray/duty/obligation]
Feebly/faint/bit-by-bit
[Appear/come-into-sight/are-wholly/wash] [cross-over/extend/span]
[Swallows/rapids/Zeze] 's [net replace wood = fishing basket stakes]

Ajiroji are stakes of bamboo with baskets attached, stuck into the river to catch fish. "Seze" means shallows or rapids whereas "zeze" is the name of the place where the Uji River flows out of Lake Biwa. Different texts use either reading for this poem.

小倉擬百人一首
相模

#65 Lady Sagami, "Bitter grieving"

Translation

By Lady Sagami (998-1061)

Bitter grieving
And my sleeves will not dry—
But the rot
Of our love is not so bad
As that of my name.

Original Japanese	Pronunciation
相模	Sagami
恨みわび	Urami wabi
ほさぬ袖だに	Hosanu sode da ni
あるものを	Aru mono wo
恋に朽ちなん	Koi ni kuchinan
名こそ惜しけれ	Na koso oshi kere

Literal Notes

[Resentment/bitterness] [worried/grieved/pined-for/apology/refinement]
Drying not sleeve even
Is [although(with strong nuance of discontent)/but/even-though/I-wish]
Love to rot
Name/reputation that regrettable/precious/dear/too-good-for

Sleeves being wet is a poetic symbol of wiping off tears. Thus, sleeves being unable to dry means crying nonstop.

小倉擬百人一首

#66 High Priest Gyouson, "Together in pity and sorrow"

Translation

By High Priest Gyouson (1055-1135)

Together
In pity and sorrow,
My mountain cherry—
Besides your flowers
There is no one.

Original Japanese	**Pronunciation**
大僧正行尊	Daisoujou Gyouson
もろともに	Morotomo ni
哀れと思へ	Aware to omoe
山桜	Yama-zakura
花より外に	Hana yori hoka ni
知る人もなし	Shiru hito mo nashi

Literal Notes

Together
Pity/sorrow/grief feeling
Mountain cherry
Flower than besides/in-addition-to/other
Know person also/there-is none [know person = friends, acquaintances]

In "morotomo," "tomo" by itself can be read as "friend." Gyouson wrote this poem after wandering in the mountain and encountering a lovely cherry blossom. Both he and the cherry blossom were all alone, except for each other.

百人一首之内 周防内侍

#67 Lady Suou no Naishi, “How regrettable it would be”

Translation

By Lady Suou no Naishi (1037-1109)

On a short spring night
To rest amid your arms
Is but a dream—
How regrettable it would be
To ruin my name so pointlessly.

Original Japanese	**Pronunciation**
周防内侍	Suou no Naishi
春の夜の	Haru no yo no
夢ばかりなる	Yume bakari naru
手枕に	Tamakura ni
かひなく立たむ	Kainaku tatan
名こそ惜しけれ	Na koso oshi kere

Literal Notes

Spring ’s night ’s [= short spring night]
Dream [just/merely/nothing-but/approximately] had/became
Hand pillow [= using arm as a pillow]
[Worthless/pointless/not-keep/without-deserving] [stand-out]
Name/reputation that [regrettable/dear/too-good-for/almost-not-quite] is

Lady Suou no Naishi was tired one night at the royal court and expressed a wish for a pillow. One of the male courtiers offered his arm through the separation screen. She composed this poem as a response, meaning that she would not ruin her reputation in such a pointless way.

小倉擬百人一首
三條院

#68 Retired Emperor Sanjou, "If I stay long..."

Translation

By Retired Emperor Sanjou (976-1017)

My heart, my will,
So roughly treated,
A floating world—
But if I stay long
I'll yearn for the midnight moon

Original Japanese	**Pronunciation**
三条院	Sanjou In
心にも	Kokoro ni mo
あらで浮世に	Arade ukiyo ni
ながらへば	Nagaraeba
恋しかるべき	Koishikaru beki
夜半の月かな	Yowa no tsuki kana

Literal Notes

Heart/will
[Crude/rough/flaw] [floating-world/fleeting-world/transitory-world/sad-life]
[Though/notwithstanding/during/while/both OR long-if]
Yearn-for/miss should
Midnight/dead-of-night 's moon how!/alas!

It is said that the retired Emperor Sanjou wrote this poem upon his forced abdication, resulting from the powerful Fujiwara family taking control. He thought he would not live long in this world, but if he should be forced to live in the sad world a long time, he did not want to be reminded of his happy former life, symbolized by the midnight moon.

百人一首之内 能因法師

#69 Monk Nouin, “A tempest crudely blows”

Translation

By Monk Nouin (~ 988-1050)

A tempest crudely blows
The maples and leaves
Of Mount Mimuro—
Making the Tatsuta River
A fine brocade

Original Japanese	Pronunciation
能因法師	Nouin Houshi
あらし吹く	Arashi fuku
三室の山の	Mimuro no yama no
もみぢ葉は	Momijiba wa
龍田の川の	Tatsuta no kawa no
にしきなりけり	Nishiki nari keri

Literal Notes

Storm/tempest/crude/rough blows/gust
Mimuro ’s mountain ’s
Maple leaves
Tatsuta ’s river/stream ’s
Brocade became(personal recollection or something heard)

Although there are mountains named Mimuro and a river named Tatsuta in the Yamato region, they are not located close enough for this scene to have actually happened, suggesting it is a work purely of the poet’s imagination.

百人一首之内　良暹法師

#70 Monk Ryouzen, "Loneliness"

Translation

By Monk Ryouzen (active ~ 1038-1065)

Loneliness—
I leave my hut
And gaze around;
But everywhere's the same
In autumn twilight

Original Japanese	**Pronunciation**
良暹法師	Ryouzen Houshi
寂しさに	Sabishisa ni
宿を立出て	Yado wo tachi idete
ながむれば	Nagamureba
いづこもおなじ	Izuko mo onaji
秋の夕暮	Aki no yugure

Literal Notes

Loneliness/desolation
Shelter/lodging stand leave
[Look-around/gaze-far-off] when
[Where/what-place/everywhere] [same/alike/changeless]
Autumn 's evening/twilight

#71 Minamoto no Tsunenobu, "Blown by autumn wind"

Translation

By Chief Counselor Tsunenobu, Minamoto no Tsunenobu (1016-1097)

When it's evening
The leaves visit
My hut of reeds
From Kadota,
Blown by autumn wind

Original Japanese	**Pronunciation**
大納言經信	Dainagon Tsunenobu
夕されば	Yu sareba
門田の稲葉	Kadota no inaba
おとづれて	Otozurete
あしのまろやに	Ashi no maroya ni
秋風ぞふく	Akikaze zo fuku

Literal Notes

Evening when
Kadota/gate+rice-field 's rice-plant pieces/leaves
[Having-visited/called-on/arrived/appeared/knocked-on/"Oto" = sound]
[Foot/leg/reed/bullrush] 's/of round hut to/into
Autumn wind/breeze blows

百人一首之内 祐子内親王家紀伊

#72 Lady Yushi Naishinno-ke no Kii, "Coquettish waves"

Translation

By Lady Yushi Naishinno-ke no Kii (1087-1109)

I've heard the sound
Of Takeshi Beach's
Coquettish waves
But I will not venture
Lest I wet my sleeves.

Original Japanese	Pronunciation
祐子内親王家紀伊	Yushi Naishinno-ke no Kii
音にきく	Oto ni kiku
高師の浜の	Takashi no hama no
あだ浪は	Adanami wa
かけじや袖の	Kakeji ya sode no
ぬれもこそすれ	Nure mo koso sure

Literal Notes

Sound hear [i.e., know their fame]
Takashi 's beach 's
[Vain/futile/foe/enemy/coquettish-woman] wave
[Soar/fly/run/dash/wage/risk/gamble] no and sleeve
Wet this/indeed do/be

Takashi Beach is near Osaka and was famous for its waves. "Ada" means "vain/futile" but can also be "coquettish woman," thus a wordplay symbolizing flirtation. However, the waves come and go, thus her suitor is not reliable. Sleeves are an emblem of love and wetting the sleeves is a common Japanese poetic symbol for wiping off the tears.

小倉擬百人一首
前中納言
匡房

#73 Oe no Masafusa, “Do not suppress my view”

Translation

By Counselor Masafusa, Oe no Masafusa (1041-1111)

On the slope
Beneath the mountain peak
The cherries bloom—
Oh nearby mountain mist,
Do not suppress my view!

Original Japanese

権中納言匡房

高砂の
尾の上の桜
咲きにけり
外山の霞
たたずもあらなん

Pronunciation

Gon Chuunagon Masafusa

Takasago no
Onoe no sakura
Saki ni keri
Toyama no kasumi
Tatazu mo aranan

Literal Notes

Takasago/high-sand ’s [= a place name *or* a pillow word associated with mountain summits]
[Tail/end/lower-slope-of-a-mountain] ’s above ’s cherry-tree
Blossom/bloom have
[Nearby-mountain/mountain-near-human-settlement] ’s haze/mist
[Stand/erect/pass/sever/cut-off/suppress/rise-up] no also do-not

小倉擬百人一首
源俊頼朝臣
鳴神上人
豊国画

#74 Minamoto no Toshiyori, "Not exactly what I was praying for..."

Translation

By Courtier Minamoto no Toshiyori (1055-1129)

Coldheartedly
She blows Hatsuse's
Mountain storm
With more ferocity—
Not exactly what I was praying for...

Original Japanese	Pronunciation
源俊頼朝臣	Minamoto no Toshiyori Ason
うかりける	Ukari keru
人をはつせの	Hito wo Hatsuse no
山おろし	Yama oroshi
はげしかれとは	Hageshikare to wa
祈らぬものを	Inoranu mono wo

Literal Notes

Carelessly/thoughtlessly/inadvertently/unkind is
Person [Hatsuse/beginning-torrents] 's/of
Mountain [wind-storm/fall/precipitate/go-down]
[Violent/fierce/tempestuous] [he/become-hoarse/wither/blast] that
Pray/wish did not [although (with strong discontent)/but/I-wish]

Hatsuse is a temple near Nara and a common place for lovers to go and pray. It is known for its storms, hence the *kanji* in its name meaning "beginning torrent." In this poem, he is comparing his lover's fury with that of the storms of Hatsuse, giving an ironic contrast between the prayers for happiness and the coldness of the fury; he loves her but she does not care for him at all.

小倉擬百人一首
藤原基俊

#75 Fujiwara no Mototoshi, "This year too shall pass"

Translation

By Fujiwara no Mototoshi (1060-1142)

You made a pledge
With life like dew
Upon a plant:
Alas, another autumn
And this year too shall pass

Original Japanese

藤原基俊

契りをきし
させもが露を
命にて
あはれことしの
秋もいぬめり

Pronunciation

Fujiwara no Mototoshi

Chigiri okishi
Sasemo ga tsuyu wo
Inochi ni te
Aware kotoshi no
Aki mo inumeri

Literal Notes

Pledge [greatly/do/put/place/leave(behind)/get-up/rise/occur]
[Moxa-plant/mugwort/point/pledge/pierce/prick/insert/shine/tinged] dew
Mortal-life
[Sorrow/grief/pity/Alas!/meet/encounter] this year 's
Autumn also [about-to-pass]

This poem refers to a promise made and broken by the Regent to promote his son to a higher office. He is comparing the promise to dew on *sasemo*, a type of herbal plant similar to mugwort.

小倉擬百人一首
法性寺入道前関白太政大臣

#76 Fujiwara no Tadamichi, “A sky of waves in frothy white”

Translation

By Hosshou Temple Lay Priest/Retired Prime Minister,
Fujiwara no Tadamichi (1097-1164)

Coming out
From ocean plains
The sky and clouds appear—
But I wonder... the distant sea...
A sky of waves in frothy white

Original Japanese	**Pronunciation**
法性寺入道関白太政大臣	Hosshouji no Nyuudou Kanpaku Dajoudaijin
わたの原	Wata no hara
こぎ出でて見れば	Kogi idete mireba
久方の	Hisakata no
雲井にまよふ	Kumoi ni mayou
おきつしらなみ	Okitsu shiranami

Literal Notes

Sea/cotton/guts/bowels ’s field/plain
[To-go-out] see/view when
Sky/moon ’s
[Sky/cloud/distant-place/imperial-court] [waver/hesitate/lose-control]
[Open-sea/rise-high-into-sky] [white-waves/wavecaps]

Fujiwara no Tadamichi was Prime Minister during the Hougen Rebellion (1156) in which his faction won. He was known for his intrigues and later retired to the Houshou Buddhist temple and became a lay priest.

百人一首之内
崇徳院

#77 Retired Emperor Sutoku, "These rapids shall meet again"

Translation

Poem By Retired Emperor Sutoku (1119-1164)

A torrent abrupt
Is torn by rocks
And though it's smashed
This broken brook
Shall meet again

Original Japanese

崇徳院御製

瀬をはやみ
岩にせかるる
滝川の
われても末に
逢はむとぞ思ふ

Pronunciation

Sutoku In Gyosei

Se wo hayami
Iwa ni sekaruru
Takigawa no
Warete mo sue ni
Awan to zo omou

Literal Notes

[Shallows/rapids/position/chance] [at-once/immediately/quick-see]
Rock/crag [blocked-up/compete/torrent/rapids/continuously]
Rapids/cascade
[Break/smash/divided] [though/even-if] [finally/after/following]
Meet/rendezvous do think/feel

"Gyosei" means a poem written by the emperor. Emperor Sutoku was on the losing side of the Hougen Rebellion and forced into exile afterward. In exile, he lived a monastic life, studying Buddhist scripture.

百人一首之内 源兼昌

#78 Minamoto no Kanemasa, "Singing voices"

Translation

By Minamoto no Kanemasa (active ~ 1100-1128)

Singing voices,
The Awaji Island pipers
Going back and forth—
How many sleepless nights
For the Suma gatekeeper?

Original Japanese	**Pronunciation**
源兼昌	Minamoto no Kanemasa
淡路島	Awaji shima
かよふ千鳥の	Kayou chidori no
なく声に	Naku koe ni
いくよねざめぬ	Ikuyo nezamenu
すまの関守	Suma no sekimori

Literal Notes

Awaji Island
[Commute/back-and-forth/song/ballad/in-such-a-way] plover/sandpiper 's
[Sing/cry-out/weep/not-having] voice
[Generations/ages/years/number-of-nights/go] sleep not
Suma gatekeeper

The Suma barrier gate is near Kobe and across from Awaji Island. The poet is said to have written this poem after spending the night there and hearing the beach birds' cries. Exiled officials frequently went to Awaji Island and the Suma Barrier was featured in the classic story, the *Tale of Genji*.

百人一首之内 左京大夫顕輔

#79 Fujiwara no Akisuke, "Lingering in autumn wind"

Translation

By Vice Minister Akisuke, Fujiwara no Akisuke (1090-1155)

Shining moonlight
Seeps through
Rifts of clouds—
Its shadow lingering
In autumn wind

Original Japanese	**Pronunciation**
左京大夫顕輔	Sakyou no Daibu Akisuke
秋風に	Akikaze ni
たなびく雲の	Tanabiku kumo no
たえまより	Taema yori
もれ出づる月の	More izuru tsuki no
かげのさやけさ	Kage no sayakesa

Literal notes

Autumn wind
[Linger/hover-above/trail/hang-over/spread-about] cloud 's
Interval/gap/rifts than/from
[Come-through/shine-through/protect/keep-promise] go-out moon 's
Shadow/silhouette/reflection/light 's [clearness/brightness]

小倉擬百人一首
待賢門院堀川

#80 Lady Horikawa, “My hair and feelings are both in tangles”

Translation

By Empress Dowager Taiken, Lady Horikawa (active ~ 1142)

I do not know
The constancy of his heart—
And this morning
My hair and feelings
Are both in tangles

Original Japanese

待賢門院堀河

長からむ
心もしらず
黒髪の
みだれてけさは
物をこそ思へ

Pronunciation

Taiken Moin no Horikawa

Nagakaran
Kokoro mo shirazu
Kurokami no
Midarete kesa wa
Mono wo koso omoe

Literal Notes

Long-time
Heart also know not
Black hair ’s
[Disordered/disarrayed/chaos/disheveled/confused] this-morning
Thing this feeling

“Midarete” literally means “black hair” but is a “pillow word” for “disordered, confused, tangled.”

#81 Fujiwara no Sanesada, "Cuckoo"

Translation

By Minister of the Left Tokudaiji, Fujiwara no Sanesada (1139-1191)

Cuckoo—
I look in the
Singing sound's direction
But only the morning
Moon remains

Original Japanese	**Pronunciation**
後徳大寺左大臣	Go Tokudaiji no Sadaijin
ほととぎす	Hototogisu
鳴きつる方を	Nakitsuru kata wo
眺むれば	Nagamureba
ただ有明の	Tada ariake no
月ぞのこれる	Tsuki zo nokoreru

Literal Notes

Cuckoo
Cry/sing has direction
Stare/watch/see when
Just/only early-dawn/daybreak 's
Moon remain

The Japanese cuckoo, not related to the European cuckoo, only cries once or twice a day, around sunrise or sunset. As people hear but do not see the bird, a poetic legend has it that the bird is coming from the spirit world to warn the farmers that it is time to sow rice. Another legend has it that the bird's singing is inviting a tryst that will lead to the underworld.

百人一首
道因法師

#82 Monk Douin, "Grieving though life remains"

Translation

By Monk Douin (1090-1182)

Grieving
Though life
Remains
And sadness cannot
Contain the tears

Original Japanese	Pronunciation
道因法師	Douin Houshi
思ひわび	Omoi wabi
さても命は	Satemo inochi wa
あるものを	Aru mono wo
憂きに堪へぬは	Uki ni taenu wa
なみだなりけり	Namida nari keri

Literal Notes

Think/feel worried/grieved/pine-for
Although mortal-life/fate/destiny
Is/exists [although (with discontent)/but/even-though/I-wish...]
Melancholy/grief/sad withstand/endure not
Tears are/have become

#83 Fujiwara no Toshinari, "A deer cries"

Translation

By Empress Dowager Steward, Fujiwara no Toshinari (1114-1204)

Society's midst
A tearful path,
Desiring retreat
To mountain depths—
But there too, a deer cries.

Original Japanese

皇太后宮大夫俊成

世の中よ
道こそなけれ
思ひ入る
山のおくにも
鹿ぞ鳴くなる

Pronunciation

Koutaigouguu no Daibu Toshinari

Yo no naka yo
Michi koso nakere
Omoi iru
Yama no oku ni mo
Shika zo naku naru

Literal Notes

World/age/era 's midst [= society/the-world/the-times]
Path/road/Buddhist-Path this [not-there-is/shed-tears]
Feeling/though enter/joins [= retiring into thoughts or the mountain]
Mountain 's heart at also
Deer cries

The poet ended up becoming a Buddhist priest. A deer's cry is symbolic of sadness. Although it is not written with the *kanji*, the pronunciation of "naku naru" can also mean "pass away."

小倉擬百人一首
藤原清輔朝臣

#84 Fujiwara no Kiyosuke, "If I live long I may reminisce"

Translation

By Counselor Fujiwara no Kiyosuke (1104-1177)

If I live long
I may reminisce
Of this time too;
For now I miss that age
When I saw the world in fear

Original Japanese	Pronunciation
藤原清輔朝臣	Fujiwara no Kiyosuke Ason
ながらへば	Nagaraeba
またこの頃や	Mata konogoro ya
しのばれむ	Shinobaren
憂しと見し世ぞ	Ushi to mishi yo zo
今は恋しき	Ima wa koishiki

Literal Notes

[Long/though/while/notwithstanding/during] when/if
Then/again [recently/this-time]
Recollect/long-for/conceal-oneself/endure shall
Anxiety see world/society/generation
Now miss/yearn-for/love

小倉擬百人一首
俊恵法師

#85 Monk Shun'e, "Even the bedroom shutters are heartless"

Translation

By Monk Shun'e (1113-1191?)

All night
An anxious night
A sun that does not rise:
For even the bedroom shutters
Are heartless

Original Japanese

俊恵法師

夜もすがら
物思ふ頃は
明けやらぬ
ねやのひまさへ
つれなかりけり

Pronunciation

Shun'e Houshi

Yo mo sugara
Mono omou koro wa
Ake yaranu
Neya no hima sae
Tsure nakari keri

Literal Notes

Night all/throughout
Anxiety time/while/during as-for
Dawn/sunrise/daybreak do-not
[Sleep-room/bedroom] [free-time/farewell/intervals] [even/clear/crisp]
[Companion/lead/take/hang/suspend/cramped not (=heartless)] is

This poem alludes to waiting for a lover that does not come while the shutters also keep out the sunlight, making the night even longer.

#86 Monk Saigyou, "What an excuse"

Translation

By Monk Saigyou (1118-1190)

"Lament!"
Says the moon
As I ponder things—
But what an excuse
For the tears of my troubled face

Original Japanese

西行法師

なげけとて
月やは物を
思はする
かこちがほなる
わがなみだかな

Pronunciation

Saigyou Houshi

Nageke tote
Tsuki ya wa mono wo
Omowasuru
Kakochi gao naru
Waga namida kana

Literal Notes

[Sigh/lament/grieve] say
Moon and thing
Think/feel/thinking-over do
[Complain-about/grumble/make-excuse-for/troubled] face is/become
I/my tears/cries how!/alas!

#87 Monk Jakuren, "The misty fog goes up through pines"

Translation

By Monk Jakuren (1139?-1202)

A passing shower's
Dew as yet undried—
The misty fog
Goes up through pines
In autumn twilight

Original Japanese

寂蓮法師

むらさめの
露もまだひぬ
まきの葉に
霧立ちのぼる
秋の夕暮

Pronunciation

Jakuren Houshi

Murasame no
Tsuyu mo mada hinu
Maki no ha ni
Kiri tachinoboru
Aki no yugure

Literal Notes

Passing-shower 's
[At-all/in-the-least/the-least-bit/dew/tears/drops] also until/yet dry-not
[Plum-pine/sow/plant/seed/scatter/sprinkle/strew/wind/coil/roll] leaf to
Fog/mist go-up/rise-up
Autumn 's evening/twilight

Autumn's evening is a seasonal poetic symbol of loneliness and dreariness and rain drops are symbolic of tear drops. Maki is a plum pine but is also used for pines in general. "Maki" can also be read as "scatter" or "sprinkle" so you can read the third line as the pine's needles are scattered while the fog rises up through the trees.

小倉擬百人一首
皇嘉門院別当

#88 Attendant to Empress Kouka, "Must I devote myself...?"

Translation

By an Attendant to Empress Kouka (active ~ 1175-1182)

A reed cut-off from
Naniwa Bay—
Must I devote myself
For wading into
Passion that night?

Original Japanese	**Pronunciation**
皇嘉門院別当	Kouka Moin no Betto
難波江の	Naniwae no
芦のかりねの	Ashi no karine no
一夜ゆへ	Hitoyo yue
身をつくしてや	Mi wo tsukushite ya
恋わたるべき	Koi wataru beki

Literal Notes

Naniwa Bay 's
Reeds 's cut-(reed)/nap/temporary 's
[One-night/all-night/one-joint] [reason/cause/circumstance/fasten/fix]
[Body/self] [relying-entirely-on/using-solely/exhausting/all-sorts/all-kinds]
[Love/tender-passion] [pass/cross-over/wade] must

Naniwa was the ancient name for Osaka and Naniwa Bay was a famous place for lovers to meet. It was also famous for the growth of rushes. This poem was written on the topic of "love at a travel inn."

This tanka is heavy with wordplay. "Karine" can mean either a nap or the cut stump of a reed. "Hitoyo" can either mean one night or one joint of a rush. "Mi wo tsukushite" can either mean exhausting yourself or a water measuring gauge.

小倉擬百人一首
式子内親王
久松
おそめ

#89 Princess Shokushi, "A string of pearls"

Translation

By Princess Shokushi (1149-1201)

A string of pearls—
If life dies out, die now;
If I live long
Concealing my feelings,
I weaken so.

Original Japanese	**Pronunciation**
式子内親王	Shokushi Naishinnou
玉の緒よ	Tama no wo yo
絶えなば絶えね	Taenaba taene
ながらへば	Nagaraeba
しのぶることの	Shinoburu koto no
よはりもぞする	Yowari mo zo suru

Literal Notes

Ball/sphere 's string/cord [=bead string, thread of life]
[Dying-out/petering-out/becoming-extinct] if [ceasing/cut-off]
[Live-long-time/though/notwithstanding/while] when/while/if
Conceal-oneself/hide/endure/recollect/fern/hair-style thing 's
Weaken/downcast/dejected/perplexed also do

#90 Attendant to Empress Inpu, "The Male Island's female divers"

Translation

By Attendant to Empress Inpu (1130-1200)

Look!
The Male Island's female divers—
Their sleeves are wet,
So thoroughly wet,
The color cannot change.

Original Japanese	**Pronunciation**
殷富門院大輔	Inpu Monin no Taiyuu
見せばやな	Misebaya na
雄島のあまの	Ojima no ama no
袖だにも	Sode dani mo
ぬれにぞぬれし	Nure ni zo nureshi
色はかはらず	Iro wa kawarazu

Literal Notes

Look/see when/if hey!
[Male Island = Ojima] 's [heaven/sky/female-shell-diver/sweet/rain] 's
Sleeve/wing is on
Wet through ! wet again
Color change not

Wet sleeves is a frequent Japanese poetical symbol of tears, hinting at heartbreak from love.

小倉擬百人一首
後京極摂政前太政大臣
清玄尼

#91 Fujiwara no Yoshitsune, "Must I sleep alone?"

Translation

By Prime Minister and Regent Go-Kyougoku, Fujiwara no Yoshitsune (1169-1206)

A cricket chirps
A frosty night
A mat of cold and white—
It holds a folded robe
But must I sleep alone?

Original Japanese	Pronunciation
後京極摂政太政大臣	Go-Kyougoku no Sesshou Dajoudaijin
きりぎりす	Kirigirisu
鳴くや霜夜の	Naku ya shimo yo no
さむしろに	Samushiro ni
衣かたしき	Koromo katashiki
ひとりかも寝む	Hitori kamo nen

Literal Notes

Grasshopper/cricket
Cry/sing/sound/chirp frost-night 's
[Samu=cold; mushi=bug; mushiro= straw-mat/instead; shiro=white] on
Clothes/garment/robe/coating [direction style = folding]
Alone [? how/might] sleep

The third line could read many different ways, with "samu" being cold and "mushiro" being "straw mat" as the two main readings. However, with the additional meanings of "bug" (referring to the cricket) and "white," it allows the poem to be read in two ways. The first way, the poet is sleeping alone on his straw mat listening to a cricket chirp in the frosty night. The second way refers to a lone cricket chirping on bed coated in white (i.e., snow).

小倉擬百人一首
二條院 讃岐

#92 Lady Sanuki, "He is one that does not know"

Translation

By Retired Emperor Nijou's Attendant, Lady Sanuki (1141-1217)

My sleeve
A rock from open sea,
Unseen though tide is low—
For he is one that does not know
There is no time for it to dry.

Original Japanese	**Pronunciation**
二条院讃岐	Nijou In no Sanuki
わが袖は	Waga sode wa
潮干に見えぬ	Shiohi ni mienu
沖の石の	Oki no ishi no
人こそしらね	Hito koso shirane
かはくまもなし	Kawaku ma mo nashi

Literal Notes

I/my/peace/calm sleeve
[Low-tide or (tide/salt-water/opportunity dry)] [see/hope/chances/idea] not
[Okinoishi or (open-sea/rise-high-to-sky 's rock/stone)] 's
Person that know not
[Thirsty/dry] [space/time/interval/moment] also [without/achieve/change]

Wet sleeves are a symbol of sadness or a broken heart as they're used to wipe off tears.

小倉擬百人一首
鎌倉右大臣

#93 Minamoto no Sanetomo, "A shore to paddle to"

Translation

By Minister of the Right Kamakura, Minamoto no Sanetomo (1192-1219)

Among the world
I long for harbor,
A shore to paddle to—
But how sad it is...
The mooring rope of heaven's boat

Original Japanese	**Pronunciation**
鎌倉右大臣	Kamakura no Udaijin
世の中は	Yo no naka wa
つねにもがもな	Tsune ni mo ga mo na
なぎさこぐ	Nagisa kogu
あまの小舟の	Ama no obune no
綱手かなしも	Tsuna de kanashi mo

Literal Notes

World/age/era 's midst [= society/the-world/the-times]
Harbor/port/ferry [speaker's hope, desire, wish]
[Water's-edge/beach/shore/calm] [row/paddle/push-through/pull-roots]
[Heaven/imperial/male-diver/female-shell-diver/sweet] boat/small-craft
Mooring-rope [sad/sorrowful too or (alas!/how! is too)]

小倉擬百人一首
参議雅経
一勇斎国芳画

#94 Fujiwara no Masatsune, "The beating of the robes"

Translation

By Counselor Masatsune, Fujiwara no Masatsune (1170-1221)

Seeing Yoshino—
The mountain's autumn wind
Blowing as the night grows old
My hometown cold
The beating of the robes

Original Japanese	Pronunciation
参議雅経	Sangi Masatsune
みよし野の	Miyoshino no
山の秋風	Yama no akikaze
さよふけて	Sayo fukete
ふるさとさむく	Furusato samuku
衣うつなり	Koromo utsu nari

Literal Notes

[Viewing/spectacle] Yoshino 's
Mountain 's autumn/fall breeze
Evening get-late/wear-on/blowing
Old-village/hometown cold
[Clothes/robe/garments] [hit/beat/strike/depression/low-spirits] is/become

The beating of the robes refers to the old way of washing clothes and hanging them in the wind. Autumn wind is a gloomy and lonely symbol while "utsu" can have a double meaning of "depression."

小倉擬百人一首
前大僧正慈圓
大伴黒主
應需 豊国画

#95 Former High Priest Jien, "My black sleeves, a cold shoulder"

Translation

By Former High Priest Jien (1155-1225)

Receiving not
The people of this floating world,
A burden I carry...
Cut off from former times
My black sleeves... a cold shoulder.

Original Japanese

前大僧正慈円

おほけなく
うき世の民に
おほふかな
わがたつそまに
墨染の袖

Pronunciation

Saki no Daisoujou Jien

Ookenaku
Ukiyo no tami ni
Oou kana
Waga tatsu soma ni
Sumizome no sode

Literal Notes

Receive/catch not
[Floating/merry/gossip/rumor/scandal/bad-reputation/rainy-season]
[world/society/age] 's [citizen/people/nation] to
[Chase/cover/hide/conceal/bear/drive/expel/carry-on-back] how!/alas!
[Me/I/harmony/peace] [stand/build/pass/elapse/sever/cut-off/abstain]
[while/during/sparse-time/former-times]
Black-ink dye/color/stain/print 's sleeve/give-someone-cold-shoulder

"Ukiyo" is the "floating world" or the merry, pleasure-seeking urban life, but also has the connotation of being empty, seeking pleasures in a fleeting and transient life. Here, "uki" is written in the *hiragana* alphabet rather than in the *kanji* ideagram, leaving it open to other meanings, including scandal, bad reputation, and rainy season.

"Black sleeves" denotes the black garb of priests. He is referring to turning away from the meaningless, pleasure-seeking world of society and his former life and going on a more spiritual path.

小倉擬百人一首
入道前太政大臣

#96 Fujiwara no Kintsune, "Perhaps... it was me?"

Translation

By Priest and Former Prime Minister, Fujiwara no Kintsune (1171-1244)

Flowers pointing
To garden snow
That vanished in the storm,
Passing away:
Perhaps... it was me?

Original Japanese	Pronunciation
入道前太政大臣	Nyuudou Saki no Dajoudaijin
花さそふ	Hana sasou
あらしの庭の	Arashi no niwa no
雪ならで	Yuki nara de
ふりゆくものは	Furi yuku mono wa
わが身なりけり	Waga mi nari keri

Literal Notes

Flower [invite/ask/tempt/point/pierce/insert/shine/leads]
[Storm/tempest/lay-waste] 's garden 's
Snow not-being
[Falling/pass/disadvantage] go/pass-away thing
My body/self [was-it?/was-not-it?]

#97 Fujiwara no Teika, "Boiling salt from water"

Translation

By Counselor Sadaie, Fujiwara no Teika (1162-1241)

She is not coming
To Matsuo Bay—
And in the evening calm
They're boiling salt from water
As I'm yearning

Original Japanese

権中納言定家

こぬ人を
まつほの浦の
夕なぎに
やくやもしほの
身もこがれつつ

Pronunciation

Gon Chuunagon Sadaie

Konu hito wo
Matsuo no ura no
Yunagi ni
Yaku ya moshio no
Mi mo kogare tsutsu

Literal Notes

Come not person
[Matsuo/wait/bubble/end] Bay
Evening calm to/at
[Burn/boil/use/service/misfortune/disaster/jealous/about] [seaweed/mourning] [salt/salt-water/sea-water/tide/ebb-and-flow/opportunity]
Body/self also [yearn-for/be-in-love-with/get-impatient/irritated/pull-up-by-roots]

Sadaie was the compiler of this anthology, *Hyakunin Isshu*, and was a renowned poet and editor of his era. "Matsu" has the double meaning of "to wait," so he was waiting for a lover that did not show.

小倉擬百人一首
正三位家隆
揚帳

#98 Fujiwara no Ietaka, "A sign of summer cleansing"

Translation

By Official Ietaka, Fujiwara no Ietaka (1158-1237)

Rustling wind
In oaks by Nara's brooks—
This evening
I see a sign
Of summer cleansing

Original Japanese	Pronunciation
従二位家隆	Junii Ietaka
風そよぐ	Kaze soyogu
ならの小川の	Nara no ogawa no
夕ぐれは	Yugure wa
みそぎぞ夏の	Misogi zo natsu no
しるしなりける	Shirushi nari keru

Literal Notes

Wind/breeze rustle/stir/fluttering
Nara/oak-tree 's streamlet/brook 's
Evening
[Purifying-ceremony-with-bath-of-cold-water] summer 's
[Sign-of/omen/mark/remember/know/understand] is/becomes

Wind rustling of trees is symbolic of autumn weather, fitting in with the theme of summer ending and autumn approaching.

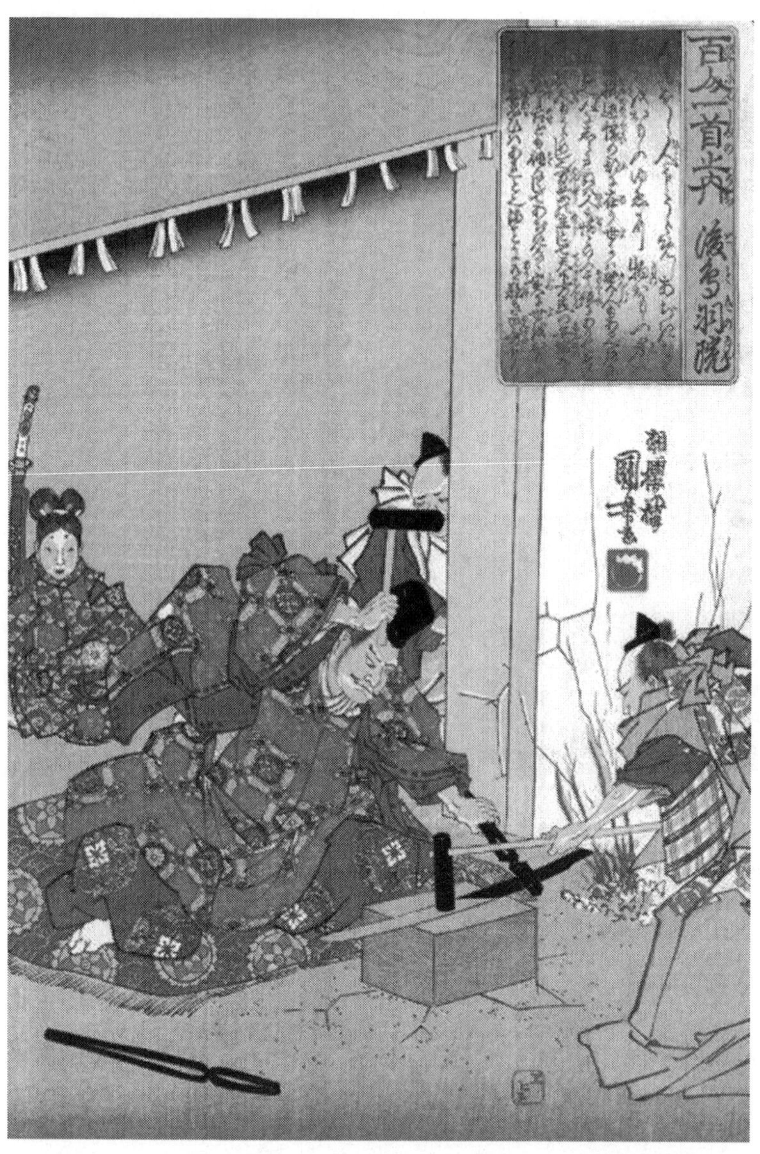

#99 Retired Emperor Gotoba, "I am weary"

Translation

Poem by Retired Emperor Gotoba (1180-1239)

I pity some
And curse the others
The flavor's gone
The worldly cares
And I am weary

Original Japanese

後鳥羽院御製

人も惜し
人も恨めし
あぢきなく
世を思ふゆゑに
もの思ふ身は

Pronunciation

Gotoba In Gyosei

Hito mo oshi
Hito mo urameshi
Ajiki naku
Yo wo omou yue ni
Mono omou mi wa

Literal Notes

Person also [regrettable/disappointing/precious/dear/too-good-for/deserving-better/almost-but-not-quite/pity]
Person also [resent/curse/blame/regret/feel-bitter/malice]
[Flavor/experience/style] [spirit/mood] not
[World/society/age] [thought/feeling] [reason/cause/circumstance]
Thing [thought/feeling/care] [body/self]

Emperor Gotoba wrote this nine years before losing his throne when he failed in an attempt to take back imperial authority from the Shogun; the Emperor remained symbolic and Gotoba was driven into exile after watching friends die in the struggle. Although the timing does not work for a commentary on losing his throne, he lived in an era of limited imperial power and constant struggles with the Shogun.

小倉擬百人一首
順徳院

#100 Retired Emperor Juntoku, "Concealed by climbing ferns"

Translation

Poem by Retired Emperor Juntoku (1197-1242)

A hundred spreading stones—
Remembering the Palace's ancient eaves
Concealed by climbing ferns;
But still, there isn't much
Of the olden days...

Original Japanese	**Pronunciation**
順徳院御製	Juntoku In Gyosei
百敷や	Momoshiki ya
古き軒端の	Furuki nokiba no
しのぶにも	Shinobu ni mo
なほあまりある	Nao amari aru
むかしなりけり	Mukashi nari keri

Literal Notes

One-hundred spreading-out/laying-out/covering [=Imperial Palace]
Old/olden eaves/edge-of-eaves
Fern/recollect/conceal/remember also
[Direct/straight/honest/simple/cheerful/furthermore/yet/still] [not-very/too-much/excess-surplus] is
[Old-times/olden-days/nothing] [was-not-it?/was-it?]

This emperor too had to abdicate his throne, but this poem was also written before then. However, it represents the feeling of how weak the imperial line was at the time, compared to the past when they had political power as well.

Made in the USA
Lexington, KY
30 January 2017